Nettie

Tales of a Brooklyn Nana

by

Peter M. Franzese

authorHOUSE™
1663 Liberty Drive, Suite 200
Bloomington, Indiana 47403
(800) 839-8640
www.AuthorHouse.com

This book is a work of non-fiction. Names of people and places have been changed to protect their privacy.

First published by AuthorHouse 11/16/04

ISBN: 1-4208-0763-3(sc)
ISBN:1-4208-0764-1 (dj)

Library of Congress Control Number: 2004098223

Printed in the United States of America
Bloomington, Indiana

This book is printed on acid-free paper.

ACKNOWLEDGMENTS

This book has been in the making now for fifteen years. It is amazing to me that this project has lasted longer than the years my Nana actually spent in my life. My journey of writing this story has been an amazing adventure in itself, which all began in September of 1989, when my then English teacher assigned us a writing project to write about a person that had a great impact on our lives. When I submitted a twenty page story to her a month later, little did I know that it was far from the ending, but really the beginning of my journey to tell the life story of my Nana.

First of all, I wish to thank my parents, Peter and Ann Marie Franzese, who from the first day of this project helped me both with their memories, and with gathering information and materials in the days when I was too young to drive and get them myself. It was their unfailing belief in my project that has gotten me to present the book before you today. Also, I thank my brother, Robert, whose interest in hearing the stories of the remarkable Nana that he does not remember inspired me to tell them. Telling him her stories over the years helped me to keep her stories alive.

Also, I wish to thank my Aunt Susan Boniface, who not only has been generous of herself, but has been at my side every step, during not only this journey, but during every one I have been on since the day I was born. She embodies everything a true godmother should be. I also thank my Uncle Anthony Lanzetta, who helped clarify the war years before the time of my mother and Aunt Susan, as well as his continued support in this project.

Although she is no longer with us, my Nana's sister, Connie Rizza deserves special recognition. Over the last twelve years of her life, Aunt Connie told and retold the Carrano family stories to me whenever I asked, whether it be at a barbecue, on the telephone, or in front of my video camera. Through her vivid and animated storytelling, she brought to life the childhood she shared with my Nana. Up until the end, as she lay dying in Our Lady of Consolation Nursing Home in West Islip, New York, Aunt Connie told many of the stories printed in this book. Then, right before her death, she said to me that her sisters were coming for her soon. She died at the age of eighty four on March 11, 2001, overjoyed that the stories of her shared childhood with Nana would be told.

There are many people who have helped me over the years with my research that made this book possible. They include the people below:

James Abramo
The late Sal Abramo
Sam & Rae Cangiano
Dominic Carrano
The late Rose Carrano
Rose Carrano
Sally Carrano

Laura Chiaino

Rose Mary Deluccio

Carmela DiGregorio

Rosa DiPaolo

Flo DiCandia

Sally Ann Fama

Julia Giovannetti

Lucille Gradante

Betty Lanzetta

Nick Lanzetta

Marie Mehrhof

The late Rose Patanjo

Katie Riceputo

Camille Smith

Carol Ann Torre of St. John's Cemetery

The late Agnes Zambrotta

Faculty of:	Our Lady of Mount Carmel rectory
	Saint Francis de Paola rectory
	Saint Cecilia rectory

Special thanks also needs to go out to my editor and friend, Jessica La Mantia, who lovingly and carefully helped me present my Nana as fresh and vivid as the great lady herself. I could not have accomplished this great fete without her.

Also I would like to express my deepest gratitude to my friends Matthew and Michael Baisley and their parents, Brian and Janice, for their love and constant support, never failing to believe in me, and their life lessons on how to "live strong." They are my heroes.

And last, but far from least, I thank Nana and Grandpa, Nettie and Bob Boniface, for the great impact they had on my life that transcends time and whose bond is stronger than death. They are still with me and helped lead me down the path to telling their story. I love you both!

For Mom, Dad and Robert with love

Table of Contents

FOREWORD

It was a few hours past her usual bedtime. At this stage of her life, Nettie's energy was sapped as the sun melted away from the sky. But on this particular night, her heart refused to let her rest. The sharp pains of angina shot through her chest and made her let out moans of agony. No, the agony of her heart would not let her rest tonight. Through pain or rest, Nettie never could spend idle time doing nothing at all. Her grandson, though only eleven, knew of her pain and suffering, and it seared his heart to see her moan and witness the agony it put her through. They both rose from their beds and went into the kitchen. After turning on the fluorescent light, Nettie sat with her grandson at the dark wood kitchen table. She opened a drawer and grabbed a handful of rubber bands.

"When I was a little girl, we used to make rubber band balls. I'm going to make one for you," she said with a smile. Although the lines in her forehead revealed the agony that she was suffering as she sat there in the kitchen, her hands began swiftly working to create a rubber band ball for her grandson to have.

As her fingers twisted the rubber bands into place, Nettie decided to take the time to sit with the grandson that idolized her and share with him the information that he wished for so desperately … the stories of her life … the tales of his Brooklyn Nana.

CHAPTER ONE

COMING TO AMERICA
1897 - 1914

In the medieval, mountainous village of Teggiano, a province of Salerno, Italy, Maria DiCandia must have been deep in thought during the spring of 1897 about the prospect of leaving behind her provincial life on her father's farm, with the hope of a better life awaiting her in the fabled land of "America," where the streets were said to be paved with gold. Maria was very unhappy at home during this spring. In November, she had turned seventeen and her step-mother, Caterina, was urging her to marry. While the prospect of marriage may not have upset Maria per say, Caterina's choice for Maria's husband upset Maria greatly. She wanted Maria to marry one of her sons, Maria's step-brother. Maria had been raised with him as a brother since she was eight-years-old. It was at that time that her own mother, Anna, died suddenly, after getting worked up over some "great worry," according to her granddaughter, Raffaela "Flo" DiCandia. Someone had made a threat against her husband, Rocco's life, and she was so consumed by this fear that her husband would be killed, this lead to her sudden and early death. Anna's death, on March twenty fifth, in either 1888 or 1889, left Rocco with six young children.

Not long after Anna's death, Rocco remarried the widow, Caterina Trezza. This woman carried the same last name as Anna's maiden name, so it is probable that she was a relative of Anna's. Caterina had children from her previous marriage, and had a daughter, Anna, named after Maria's mother, with Rocco.

While Caterina had been a kind and loving step-mother to Rocco's children, Maria's brother, Dominick, was outraged about their step-mother's marriage plans for Maria. By this time, their brother, Gerardo, and his wife, Maria, were living in Brooklyn, New York, U.S.A. Somehow, the DiCandias got word to Gerardo that they planned on making the trip across the Atlantic Ocean to join him in America. When Rocco and Caterina learned of the children's plans, they were devastated. Caterina begged Maria to reconsider her decision, but Maria's sights were set on New York.

It was a tearful goodbye as Maria bid her parents farewell. Caterina turned out dressed in black. "She mourned me for a month," Maria would tell her daughter, Nettie, many years later. Caterina knew in her heart that she would never see her step-children again. Maria also had to forever say goodbye to her younger sister, Raffaela. Raffaela had been crippled since birth and was unable to leave Teggiano. Legend has it that Maria's mother, Anna, appeared to Raffaela shortly after her death. The story that has been passed down the generations is that Rocco and the children had been working on the farm the entire day, and had completely forgotten about feeding Raffaela. When they got back to the house, they found Raffaela sitting at the table eating something. When they asked her where she had gotten the food from, she said that her mother had given it to her, and that she looked like an angel.

Leaving their parents and a few of their siblings behind, Maria and Dominick traveled fifty five miles northwest to the port in Naples, where the vessels headed for America departed from. Sometime around the beginning of June 1897, the DiCandias boarded the S.S. Oregon.

Built by Charles Connell & Company in Glasgow, Scotland in 1883, the Oregon was 360 feet long and forty feet wide. The ship had been built for the Dominion Line, under the British flag. Maria's trip to the United States was one of the ship's last voyages, as it was scrapped sometime in 1897.

With only ten dollars between the siblings after purchasing their tickets, Maria and Dominick found themselves in the damp and repulsive smelling compartment at the bottom of the boat, known as steerage class. This section, where most peasants were placed, was called "steerage" because it was located next to the deafeningly noisy steering mechanisms and engines far below the waterline. These quarters held a few hundred immigrants, where they were herded like cattle and placed in squalor where food was scare and diseases festered. The holds were rampant with illness and many passengers died before they reached New York Harbor. Of the survivors of the trip, many of them were turned away upon arrival for carrying infections diseases.

It is difficult to imagine the thoughts and emotions that filled Maria during her next three weeks at sea. Most likely, she had never left Teggiano in her life. Now she had left it behind, along with her parents, and the only life she had ever known. While she knew that the ship was headed for America and that her brother, Gerardo, was there, she could not possibly have imagined what life could have been like in the new country. I imagine that being in the company of her brother, Dominick, must have been a great comfort to her, as well as her deep and unwavering faith in the will of God. According to her niece, Flo, Rocco instilled an unshakable religious fervor in all of his children and every night in their home ended with the entire family reciting the rosary in unison on their knees on the kitchen floor. It is this religious aspect of Maria's character that she carried with her across the Atlantic. The indomitable faith of the DiCandia family survived the month-long trip across the vast ocean and down to some of the members of its future generations.

Ten days before Maria and Dominick sailed into New York Harbor, tragedy struck their final destination, Ellis Island. A fire broke out in the main building shortly after midnight on June 14, 1897, just five years after it first opened. The buildings, constructed of pine, were completely destroyed. There were 140 immigrants being held on the island at the time, but miraculously, all of them escaped unharmed, as well as all of the employees.

At the time of the tragedy, the *New York Times* described the buildings as an "old, ramshackle structure." By time the fire claimed the "ramshackle structure," approximately 1.5 million immigrants had passed through its door on their journey to begin their lives in America.

Within a month, construction began on rebuilding the main building on Ellis Island. This time fireproof materials were used, brick over a steel frame. Separate buildings contained a restaurant, laundry, bathhouse, and hospital. The Main Building was completed on June 30, 1900, but the station did not receive its first immigrants until December seventeenth of that year. The project cost a grand total of $1.5 million.

In spite of the destruction of Ellis Island, the vessels from Europe continued to arrive in New York Harbor daily, and the entry point for immigrants into America became the Barge Office on the Battery for the next three years. Unfortunately, overcrowding, lack of proper facilities, and criminals left the incoming immigrants easy targets to predators and grief.

On the feast day of Saint John the Baptist, June 24, 1897, the S.S. Oregon made its way into New York Harbor and landed at Battery Park. It is unknown the feelings that filled Maria as she looked across the water at America's majestic copper "Lady of the Harbor." It is also unknown how she finally reunited with Gerardo in New York and made her way to his home in Brooklyn. In spite of the fire that claimed the buildings on Ellis Island, 180,556 immigrants past through New York during the year of 1897.

According to the manifest of the S.S. Oregon in the records of the Ellis Island Museum, Maria and Dominick were single peasants unable to read and write. Their native tongue was Italian and their place of origin was listed as Teggiano. Their final destination was listed as “Brooklyn, joining brother Gerardo DiCandia, in Brooklyn, N.Y.”

Maria must have felt a great wave of relief at the first sight of Gerardo in this strange place. He took them to live with him in his home in Williamsburg, Brooklyn, at 7 Withers Street. In this enclave around Graham Avenue in Williamsburg, Maria must have found comfort that many of the residents in this area were not only Italian immigrants, but natives of her home province of Teggiano.

After Maria settled in Gerardo’s home, he acted as her guardian in America and in less than five months after her arrival, he was ready to marry her off. Gerardo arranged with Signora Rosa Carrano for Maria to marry her son, Cono, his friend from Teggiano. Cono was a small, stern-looking, mustached man six years Maria’s senior. Along with his widowed mother, Rosa, and three of his six siblings, Cono arrived in America from Teggiano on January 13, 1896. Rosa’s eldest child, Maria, had immigrated to the United States around 1890 for her marriage to Giuseppe Focarile. They had returned to Italy and must have regaled the Carrano family with stories of the New World across the Atlantic. Maria and Giuseppe, along with their son, Charles, came back to Brooklyn and set up residency permanently. Then Giuseppe sent for his mother-in-law and siblings-in-law and sponsored them as immigrants into the United States. In November of 1897, the Carranos were living at 23 Buschwick Avenue in Williamsburg. In that year, Rosa married off three of her children, Michael in May, Giovanna in June, and Cono in November.

While Maria escaped marrying her step-brother in Teggiano, she did not have any choice in her marriage to Cono. First you married, and then you got to know one another. Love would hopefully follow as years would pass and your brood of children continued to grow.

On November 14, 1897, Maria and Cono were married at the altar of Our Lady of Mount Carmel Church in Williamsburg. The officiating priest was Father Peter Saponara-the founding pastor of that parish-and the witnesses were Nicola Colombo and Maria Carrano.

According to the history of the parish written for its 100th anniversary in 1987, The Church of Our Lady of Mount Carmel, then on the corner of North 8th Street and Union Avenue, was built in 1887 to serve the ever growing Italian population of the Greenpoint-Williamsburg section of Brooklyn. Bishop John Loughlin, the first Bishop of Brooklyn, assigned Father Peter Saponara to establish the parish for the Italian community of Williamsburg. Saponara-who was pastor from 1887 to 1926- purchased the site of the original church for $5,000 at the corner of North 8th Street and Union Avenue. The cornerstone for the church was laid by Bishop Loughlin on July 31, 1887, and placed under the protection of Our Lady of Mount Carmel. To accommodate a larger congregation, for a still increasing parish, the original church was thrown down in 1920 and a larger church was built on the same site in 1930, only to have that church demolished in 1947 to make way for the construction of the Brooklyn-Queens Expressway, following the end of World War II. The current church of Our Lady of Mount Carmel was built in 1950 on the corner of North 8th and Havemeyer Streets, and in the rectory, till today, on a page yellowed with antiquity, is the record of the marriage of Cono Carrano to Maria DiCandia.

The early lives of Cono and Maria Carrano started out like many of their day. As the now defunct newspaper, The *Greenpoint Weekly Star* described the area in an article that appeared in the November 16, 1962 issue: "Horses clipped-clopped past fields and farms on roads paved with cobblestones, or not paved at all. There were trees everywhere . . . and the air was sweet with the scent of grass and flowers."

Maria and Cono, according to custom, began a family right away and were blessed with their first child nine months after their marriage. Their first child, a son, named Francesco (Frank), named for Cono's late father, was born on August 25, 1898. After Frank's birth, Maria and Cono moved for a short time to Rockaway, Queens. It was there that they were living when their second child, Pasquale (Pat), arrived on April 7, 1901.

In September 1901, a visitor came from Teggiano to see Maria. Rocco, along with her little brother, Cono, now fourteen, made the long journey across the ocean with the hope of bringing Maria back home. He tried to convince Maria and Cono to come back and live in Teggiano. He promised that if they returned with him, he would give them all of his land. Although Maria was probably deeply moved by her father's generous offer, she declined because she was content with her new life in America. She was now a wife and a mother and was happy to be raising her children in a place where opportunities awaited them. Yet, it is certain that it must have broken Maria's heart to break her father's. Devastated, Rocco returned to Italy alone. Maria's brother, Cono, remained in New York with his siblings. None of the DiCandia children in New York ever saw their father again. According to his granddaughter, Rosa DiPaolo, who was living in Rocco's home in Italy well into her eighties, as late as 1996, said that Rocco lived out his days on his farm and died there at the age of eighty four.

With each passing year, Maria and Cono's brood of children continued to grow. They did not remain in Rockaway and returned to live in Greenpoint. The other children they went on to have, at the rate of one every other year, were Michael in 1903, Rose, named after Cono's mother, in 1905, Vincezo (James) in 1907, Anna, named after Maria's late mother, in 1910, and Carmela in 1912. At this point, Cono and his brother-in-law, Giuseppe Focarile, had purchased the six family tenement house of 60 Kingsland Avenue in Greenpoint. The Carranos lived in a second floor apartment and the Focariles lived above them. As the year 1913 drew to a close, Maria carried her eighth child in her womb.

Cono and Maria (DiCandia) Carrano in 1937

CHAPTER TWO

GROWING UP IN THE GARDEN SPOT

1914 – 1928

Legendary author, Betty Smith, of *A Tree Grows in Brooklyn*, described the area where "Williamsburg starts to be Greenpoint" as "serene" in the summer of 1912. This description could not fit 60 Kingsland Avenue on Tuesday, September 15, 1914, as Maria's eighth child entered the world. In Maria's bedroom, the forty-year-old midwife, Pasqualina Timpanaro Abramo, delivered her fourth daughter. Right after the birth, Cono had a fight with Mrs. Abramo and she left before she had gotten around to piercing the baby's ears for earrings. This daughter of Maria's was the only one that did not have pierced ears, which was a tradition for Italian midwives to pierce the ears of infants born to the immigrants in Brooklyn during this era. Pasqualina also did not record the birth of the Carrano daughter with the City of New York, thus she never had a birth certificate, like twenty-five percent of the New York City births at that time. The only written documentation of the baby's birth is her baptismal certificate.

On the eleventh of October, Maria and Cono brought their infant daughter to the baptismal font of Our Lady of Mount Carmel for her christening. In the presence of her godparents, Vincenzo Greco and Caterina Carrano, Father Russo christened the infant, Antonia Carrano.

Antonia Carrano, born into the world on the feast day of Our Lady of Sorrows, like many children of Italian immigrants, would never be known by her Christian name. In grammar school, she was known as Antoinette, but while at home and with friends, she was simply, Nettie. Nettie was a beautiful child with a square jaw, straight chestnut hair, and large, almond eyes. In her first photograph, taken around 1923, Nettie has a wreath of white roses and a large, white bow in her hair. She carried herself with great poise, looking into the photographer's camera with a saintly countenance. As the Carrano family continued to grow, Nettie did not remain the baby of the family for long with the births of Concetta (Connie) on November 4, 1916, and Rocco on November 20, 1918.

Nettie around 1923 on her Confirmation day.

As the size of the Carrano family reached ten children by the fall of 1918, room in the second floor apartment became scarce. Not only did the children have to share bedrooms, but beds as well.

"Nettie and I slept together," her sister, Connie, remembered at the age of eighty-two in 1999. "There were two three-quarter sized beds in the room. Anna and Rosie slept by the window and Nettie and I slept by the wall. There was no furniture in the bedroom. The dining room had a chest of drawers. You couldn't even put a chair near the bed because there wasn't enough room."

While the girls slept in one room, their brother, Jimmy, slept on a folding bed in the doorway that connected the living room to the girls' bedroom.

"Jimmy would lose his temper sometimes," Connie recalled, "and one time Nettie and I were talking in bed and he was sleeping in the bed by the doorway and he said 'will you two shut up?' and we said 'stop it, we're talking' and he threw a shoe towards our bed. We got a kick out of that."

Along with the task of having to make room for the ten children to sleep, the nearly impossible task rolled around each morning of getting the little ones off to school. This task fell on the shoulders of the oldest daughter.

"Rosie was a big help to my mother because there were a lot of young ones home and she did a lot of caring for us," Connie said.

Nettie's oldest sister, Rosie, in 1924

"Rosie was like a second mother. She taught me how to walk," said Nick Lanzetta in 2003, who lived in the Carrano house from shortly after his birth in 1917.

By time Rosie was able to get herself off to school at St. Cecilia's, she was always late and tormented by the Sisters of Saint Joseph for being tardy daily. Rosie left school after the fifth grade and went out to work very early in life as a sewing machine operator.

"She was an angel of mercy … a good soul that helped everybody," Connie said. "Rosie was like a saint amongst us … she was as beautiful as the rose she was named for."

Also living under the Carrano roof around this time was Cono's intrepid widowed mother, "Mama Rosa," the nefarious character who was legendary for making trouble in her wake. Rosa Cotignola Carrano, born in Teggiano on November 15, 1853, was a pioneer in that she single-handedly uprooted her family from the poor living conditions at the time in Italy and brought her family to the United States in 1896 to escape them for a better life in a foreign land.

In the "New World," as it was dubbed by the immigrants at the turn of the twentieth century, Rosa's children married, mostly to their neighbors on Buschwick Avenue, within the first year of their immigration to America, and her grandchildren were born. Unfortunately, Rosa's feelings were so impervious, the true feelings she harbored for her family will never be known. She has been remembered as a very stern, cold, spiteful, and jealous woman. "She was a meanie," her granddaughter, Connie, said. "She lived with my mother and she made it very hard for her." Rosa never displayed an ounce of love for her children and grandchildren, leaving with them a sour impression of her to pass down to future generations.

During the time that Rosa lived with Cono and Maria, Rosa tried to bring turmoil into their home. Insanely jealous of the pious reputation that Maria held in the neighborhood, Rosa tried constantly to bring about discord in Cono and Maria's marriage. Possessing no family loyalty, Rosa attempted to spread false rumors to neighbors and family members that Maria was an unfaithful wife, that she was having an affair with a priest, which explained her constant trips to church, and that Maria had mistreated her. While she tried to coax Cono into beating Maria, Cono never doubted his wife's fidelity and goodness and ignored his mother's vicious tongue. He never laid a hand on his wife. Nor did Cono ever partake in gossip a single day of his life.

"My father never stuck up for his mother, ever," Connie said. "[Mama Rosa] couldn't wait for him to come home to tell him tales that weren't even true. My mother fed her and everything and she didn't get treated nicely by her mother-in-law."

Another time, Rosa attempted to bring discord to the Carrano household involved her namesake, Rosie. Rosa claimed that Rosie was not doing her "homework" correctly and should be punished. Homework was sewing work that women did right in the home to supply a source of income for the household. Rosa was attempting to thwart Rosie's plan of going to the movies that day, but Cono did not punish Rosie as his mother wished.

Eventually, Rosa became more of a burden than they could bear, so Cono had his mother leave his home. While none of her other children would take her into their homes either, Rosa took an apartment not far away at 12 Old Wood Point Road.

The one amusing remembrance that Nettie recalled of her "Mama Rosa" was that Rosa adored the sweet smell of fresh basil. In fact, Rosa was known for smelling of basil because she kept basil leaves in her pockets at all times. Connie remembered "Mama Rosa" as a "large woman with a bun on the top of her head." She was square-jawed and had snow white hair. Her most memorable physical attribute was the permanent scowl on her face.

Rosa saw the century she was born into draw to a close and faced the joys and sorrows, peppered with trials and tribulations, in a new century and in a new world. She witnessed the marriages of all of her seven children and the starting of their own families, making her the grandmother of approximately sixty grandchildren. Not a stranger to tragedy, Rosa was widowed at an early age; she lost her daughter, Giovanna DiCicco, from pneumonia after recently giving birth, in January of 1921, and also buried some of her grandchildren. Based on the recollections of the grandchildren who were interviewed for this book, remembering her more than seventy years after her death, Rosa probably faced these tragedies as stoically as she faced everything else.

On the morning of July 25, 1925, Rosa's son, Michael, and his wife, Katie, had recently bought their first car and brought it to Kingsland Avenue to show it off to the family. Mike was very excited to bring his mother for her first car ride. He had a day trip planned to bring her on a picnic all the way out to Lake Ronkonkoma in Suffolk County, Long Island. For the trip, he also took his niece, Jennie DeLuccio, as well as her seven-month-old son, Carmine. The group was overjoyed over the excitement of the trip, except Mama Rosa, who showed that she couldn't have cared less.

Sometime around eleven A.M., the car had made it to Bohemia, Long Island, not far from the final destination of Lake Ronkonkoma. While they were making a turn for an unknown reason, the car suddenly turned over. The windshield and windows all shattered and injured all of the passengers, except Carmine, who was protected by Jennie.

Rosa received a fatal wound from the windshield into her temple. According to her death certificate, she died from a fractured skull and shock. She was four months shy of her seventy second birthday.

The wake for the Carrano family matriarch took place in the parlor of her apartment for three days and nights. She was buried in Saint John's Cemetery in Middle Village, Queens on July 29th. Her horse-drawn hearse was followed to the cemetery by twenty six passenger cars, containing many members of her progeny.

The inscription on the black, cross-shaped, granite tombstone in section twenty would never lead a passerby to believe that "Mama Rosa" had been such a cold and despised person. In white, block letters, written in Italian, the inscription reads "In memory of our dear mother/ Rosa Carrano/died 25 July 1925/aged 72 years."

As Nettie made her entrance into the world in September of 1914, World War I had erupted in Europe. The United States did not enter the war until 1917, but when they did, her eldest brother, Frank, whom Nettie idolized from the time she was a toddler, enlisted as a seaman in the United States Navy to financially help his large family.

Nettie's oldest brother, Frank, during World War I

Frank, along with Pat, Mike, and Jimmy, had to leave school very early to go out to work to help the family. "They had to go out into the fields to pick coal and wood at five years old for my mother, and they did it," Connie said. Although Cono did well as a junkman with his pushcart through the streets of Greenpoint-Williamsburg, and Maria, along with her daughters, did homework sewing coats, they were never really financially secure. One satisfaction that they had over many families was that they owned their own home and did not have to pay rent.

Maria was given the biggest scare of her life when the family received word that Frank was missing in action. She prayed fervently for his safety and vowed that if Frank was returned to her unharmed, she would never eat meat on Wednesdays for the rest of her life.

Nettie, at the young age of four, was given a false hope when a neighbor said that she had seen Frank marching with sailors through the neighborhood. After hearing this, Nettie took off as fast as her little legs could carry her, only to find that Frank was not with them. This was the first time that Nettie remembered that she had had her hopes crushed so savagely.

Luckily, Maria's prayers were answered and Frank was found unharmed. Not long after, Frank was discharged from his service after falling from a crow's nest on the ship he was on. For the rest of her life, Maria kept the vow she made, and the hurt that Nettie felt disappeared because Frank was home at last.

In 1920, Nettie began school at Saint Cecilia's in Greenpoint in the first grade class of Sister Mary Margaret. Her education there did not last long after her sister, Carmela, was brutally beaten by her third grade nun for no apparent reason. Frank took Carmela, Nettie, and their sister, Anna, who was in the fifth grade, home from school crying. Nettie remembered her and her sisters clinging to each other crying, as Frank told the nun off and signed them out of Saint Cecilia's. He enrolled them in Public School 132 on Metropolitan

Avenue, between Manhattan Avenue and Conslyea Street, where they were no longer abused. The Carrano sisters immediately found a home at Public School 132 and grew to have a big affection for their teachers. Nettie enrolled in the 1B class of Miss Robinson. In 1989, Nettie recalled Carmela constantly fussing over her in school, making sure she had enough supplies for her classes, straightening out her collar, and making sure Nettie was presentable and prepared.

"It was a very nice school," Nettie's sister-in-law, Rose (Zambrotta) Carrano, a January 1933 graduate of Public School 132 said in 2001. "Most of the teachers were nice. It was an all girls' school. There were no boys. There were maybe forty or fifty students in a class, big classes. We had promotion twice a year."

On August 25, 1922, after having spent the day playing with her cousin, Mary DiCandia, Carmela became very ill. Dr. William Sebastian De La Hoyde of 259 Withers Street was summoned to 60 Kingsland Avenue.

Arriving with his satchel and listening tubes and pipes, De La Hoyde diagnosed Carmela with Tubercular Meningitis and quarantined the six family tenement house because of the deadly nature of the disease. Lancing pain in the head made Carmela scream into the night. Large rings must have grown around Maria's tired, sleepless eyes. She prayed at Carmela's bedside long into the night and rose before dawn to take up her rosary and pray once again.

Eighty years later, family members and friends, now well into their eighties and nineties, are haunted by the cries of indignity, as Carmela felt the sensation of nails being driven through her temples.

Childhood friend and future sister-in-law, Sally (Lanzetta) Carrano said, "[Carmela] would cry and yell and scream. She had that high fever. You would hear her scream all the time. That was the only sickness she ever had."

"I know there was a lot of commotion and something was happening," Nick Lanzetta, who lived across the hall from the Carranos, said. "They were superstitious back then and they had a rabbit in the hallway. If the rabbit lived, the person would live. If the rabbit died, the person would surely die," according to an old superstition in Brooklyn at the time, probably brought over from Europe.

All of the children that were present during Carmela's agony lost the concept of time, as the quarantine shut them out from the world, as the next ten days passed for them, probably passing unnoticed one into the next.

Nettie's sister, Carmela, on her Confirmation day in 1922

On her last day on earth, with the meningitis robbing her of her sight, Carmela's screams ceased. In her final hours on earth, with Maria keeping vigil at her bedside, Carmela revealed to her mother with great excitement the astonishing visions of heaven and the unspeakable beauty of the angels surrounding her. Then, at two A.M., on September 2, 1922, Carmela's tenth birthday, she died peacefully, with the anticipation of joining the angels that had been surrounding her bed.

James Amelia, the undertaker, took the small, lifeless body of little Carmela to prepare her to lie-in-state in the parlor that night. When that night did arrive, scores of people began arriving at the front door of 60 Kingsland Avenue, where the crepe hung on the front door. The second floor apartment was filled with mourners. Carmela was laid to rest in a diminutive, white coffin, wearing the dress that her Confirmation sponsor, Rose Dalessio, had bought for her.

Nettie remembered in 1989 her mother's uncontrollable tears and her brother, Jimmy, sitting in a folding chair at the coffin until the funeral day. When looking at the lifeless body of Carmela, Nettie was consumed by memories of Carmela being taunted by other children as they walked to school because of her "bandy legs," severely bowed legs. Also present in her mind were her memories of Carmela carefully looking after her and making sure that everything went well during her school day. Then the reality hit her, although still inconceivable - when she returned to school after the funeral was over, Carmela would never again check to see if she had a pencil or straighten her collar.

Carmela's funeral took place on September fifth. After Nettie said her final goodbye to Carmela, she went downstairs to the front of the house to line up in the funeral procession. In front of 60 Kingsland Avenue stood a white coach, pulled by white horses, awaiting Carmela's coffin.

Also assembled for the funeral procession were the girls that had made their Confirmation with Carmela that past May at Saint Francis de Paola Church. With eyes mixed with intrigue and horror, both siblings and classmates stared as the small, white coffin was carried out of the house and placed into the horse-drawn hearse. Nettie and her siblings were paired in age order and marched behind the hearse. The Confirmation girls marched on the sides of the hearse.

"There were three girls walking on each side of the hearse," Connie said. "They were all in white following the hearse to the church."

As the procession began, stretching from 60 Kingsland Avenue to Saint Francis de Paola Church on Skillman Avenue and Conslyea Street, Nettie's sister, Rose was moved by the image of the "white horses moving slowly with their heads bowed," she said in 1987. Behind the siblings and classmates marched cousins and friends.

Following the funeral mass, Carmela was laid to rest in Saint John's Cemetery in Middle Village, Queens. For thirty-five years, Carmela's final resting place was unmarked, but for the rest of her life, Maria made the journey by foot to visit her daughter's gravesite. She used statues of different saints as landmarks to lead her to the spot.

At the age of forty-five, Maria bore her eleventh and last child, on February 28, 1925. She named him Giovanni (John), although Cono wanted the baby to be named after him. He received the name John because Rosie said that Carmela had appeared to her in a dream and said that the new baby was to be called John.

Nettie's childhood on Kingsland Avenue was filled with many children, being one of ten children and having dozens of cousins in the area, and friends, such as the Lanzettas who lived in their home on the same floor since 1917. Other friends included the Gordons, the Savinos, and the Flynns, among many. This stretch of Kingsland Avenue was a very busy area during Nettie's childhood.

"Kingsland Avenue used to be cobblestone," Nick Lanzetta said. "There was a bar and grill, a saloon, Gordon and Segal's junkyard, Rose the Baker's Italian bakery, and my father's [Anthony Lanzetta's] barber shop. There was also a blacksmith shop. We used to watch the horses being shoed. Then they would herd cows down Kingsland Avenue to the slaughter house." One of the cows got away and mooed at Nettie while she played in front of her house one day.

"60 Kingsland Avenue was a six family house," Nick said. "There were the Carranos, Cono's sister and her husband, the Focariles, us, the Lanzettas, the Ragos, and the Fiumundis people."

While Nettie's family may not have lacked company, as the eighth of eleven children, she did not receive many gifts as a child. In fact, the only gifts she recalled receiving were fruit, never dolls. In 2001, at the age of ninety, Sally Lanzetta Carrano remembered meeting a three-year-old Nettie, holding a peculiar kind of makeshift doll in the backyard of the Kingsland Avenue house in 1917.

Nettie (right) with childhood chum Sally Lanzetta in Elmont, Long Island during the summer of 1927

"I first moved to 60 Kingsland Avenue when I was only six-years-old," Sally recalled. "When we had moved in, I looked into the yard and I saw Nettie. She was a little, little girl and she had a doll on her arm and she was rocking it. And guess what it was? A brick! And she had cloths wrapped around it. I was on the fire escape and I saw that and my doll was a beautiful porcelain doll with eyes that opened and closed. I showed her my doll and let her hold it and we became very good friends. We would go in and out, visiting each other all day long. We would ask questions and see what each other were doing."

Maria was always prepared for a score of unexpected visitors for dinner time. Sally claimed it was a "bottomless pot," feeding

Maria's family of twelve, her nieces on the third floor that were sure to drop by, and Sally would be invited to stay too.

When Nettie was eight years old, she was walking down Graham Avenue and spotted a porcelain doll, probably like the one that Sally had, in the store window and she fell in love with it. When she asked the owner how much it cost, he said it was fifty cents. Although by today's standards that is mere pocket change, it was a lot of money to a child from Nettie's financial background. After seeing the doll, Nettie saved every cent that came her way, until the glorious day when she saved the entire amount. She ran that day to Graham Avenue faster than she ever had in her life and bought the doll. Her dream doll was made of porcelain and had eyes that opened and closed. Nettie was never without that doll in the crook of her arm thereafter.

After Nettie had the doll for a few weeks, she took the doll to play in Cooper Park. While she was playing in the concrete bleachers, the doll slipped out of the crook of her arm and shattered into a million pieces. Nettie cried inconsolably because she had treasured that doll more than anything in the world and she had worked so hard to get it. Her brothers felt sorry for her and went to buy another one, but she said "it just wasn't the same."

About sixty-five years later, during the Christmas season of 1988, I bought a doll for my mother at our parish fair. When my Nana, Nettie, came to visit later on that Sunday, her eyes widened as she saw the doll standing on top of the mantelpiece in the living room. Immediately, she asked me where the doll had come from.

Holding the small doll in her hands, she sat down on the sofa and told firsthand the story you have just read. After hearing the story, I surprised her and gave her the doll instead. Her eyes filled with tears and she placed it under a dome on top of her dresser in her bedroom. Every morning, until the day she died, Nettie would look at that doll and smile in amazement that she had gotten the replacement to the prized doll she had lost so many years before.

By the mid-1920s, Maria and Cono's children began to marry. Frankie and Mikey married two sisters that their cousins the Focariles had introduced them to, Filomena and Antoinette. The first Carrano grandchild came along when Frank and Filomena had a daughter, Marie, named after Maria, in 1926, two years after they wed.

In 1927, the Carranos sold 60 Kingsland Avenue and moved a few blocks away to the corner, two family dwelling, 101 Beadel Street. Beadel Street, a side street off of Vandervoot Avenue, is a narrow, tree-lined block, where the houses have barely changed from the days of Nettie's childhood. "We had farmland on Beadel Street," Connie remembered, "and in the summer, Nettie and I would kick off our shoes and go barefoot through the fields there." On the property of Harper's farm, construction began in 1927 of a red and white checker-topped gas storage tank. "Nettie and I used to watch it going up every day," Connie said. A twin tank was constructed next to the first in 1946. The gas tanks became the most well-known landmark in Greenpoint-Williamsburg, until they were imploded in July of 2001.

101 Beadel Street, the Carrano home from 1927-1934

101 Beadel Street was not a tenement house, as 60 Kingsland Avenue had been. Nettie always referred to 101 Beadel Street as "my palace." In this house, there was more room, and even more privacy. There was a bathroom right in the apartment, whereas at their former home, the bathroom was a dark, airless place that was shared by the two families on the floor. "It was more countrified on Beadel Street than our previous home," Connie said.

While Cono and Maria's family occupied the bottom floor apartment, Frank and his family occupied the top floor. Nettie was all but a permanent fixture on the second floor, spending much of her time with her baby niece, Marie, and her favorite person in the world, Filomena.

Nettie with her niece Marie in 1926

"Nettie always took care of Marie," Sally said. "She watched Marie a lot. Nettie was also always with [Filomena.] They were very close. She was like a second mother to Nettie."

Besides roaming the fields of Greenpoint, Nettie and her sisters spent a great deal of their summer at their father's bungalow on Kellar Avenue in Elmont, Long Island. "Half of Greenpoint were in Elmont," Nick said. The girls went out there with friends, such as the Lanzettas, whom also had a bungalow, as well as a firework shop in the area. The Carrano sisters' favorite guests were their Uncle Emil Carrano's daughters, Aggie and Frances.

Mike and Katie Carrano, Cono's brother and sister-in-law, had property on the same block as Cono. Nettie and the girls spent a lot of time with their Aunt Katie, who was Nettie's godmother. While the girls past the summer in Elmont, Katie acted as both a guardian and a friend. She was a very much beloved aunt by all of the girls. Elmont was the girls' getaway from the hustle and bustle of city life, an escape full of "good, clean fun," as Connie said. Life in Elmont was very crude, lacking electricity and indoor plumbing. Nettie and her sisters lived the life of country girls. Although they were roughing it, Connie said that "just being together" was the most fun of all. It was a treat for Nettie to get the opportunity to spend time with her favorite cousin, Aggie, who lived in Elmhurst, Queens, not Greenpoint. She didn't get to see Aggie during the year as much as she liked. To pass the time, Nettie used to take long walks through the undeveloped, pristine area of Valley Stream, Long Island, in the times where crystal clear streams were pure and unaltered, among other breathtaking sights.

As September 1928 rolled around, Nettie was back in Greenpoint preparing for her final class at Public School 132 in the 8B, and began working on her graduation dress.

"We made our own dresses," Nettie's sister-in-law, Rose Carrano said. "We worked on them in school and then you brought it home, sometimes to finish it up, but most of the work was done at school in the sewing room. They had sewing machines in class. They taught us how to use the machines, but mostly our dresses were made by hand. You had to learn how to hem without making the stitches show on the other side. You had to start [the dress] from scratch. You had a paper pattern and pinned it on the material and cut around it. The teacher was there to supervise to show us what to do. They had a few different styles. The teacher would tell us which [style] was best for you."

While creating their white graduation dresses in sewing class was part of their day, it was only for forty minutes that they got to sew. Then the bell would ring and Nettie and her classmates were off to their next class.

"The people in your homeroom would be in all your classes," Rose said. After homeroom, the girls went off to grammar, arithmetic, drawing, sewing, and cooking. In cooking, the students were taught how to make desserts. In the 8B, Nettie's classes were now on the top floor of the three story building.

As the year 1928 drew to a close, fourteen-year-old Nettie was hard at work on her white graduation dress, her own creation with matching hat, and reflecting on her future as the era of her life at Public School 132 was drawing to a close.

CHAPTER THREE

CHILDHOOD LOVE

1929 – 1939

On the last day of January in 1929, Nettie walked to the school she had first fell in love with in the 1B, Public School 132, for the last time.

Nettie marched into the auditorium wearing the dress she had made in sewing class. "We had a beautiful auditorium and that's where the exercises were held," Rose Carrano said. "The stage was there. We sat in the seats and the principal, Miss Emily C. Powers, made a speech on the stage and the valedictorian made a speech."

According to the program written in Nettie's handwriting on the first page of her autograph book, Nettie and her "sister-grad-u-8s" began with the oath of allegiance to the flag and the singing of the "Star Spangled Banner." Other parts of the graduation included the Jumping Jack Dance, *I'll Sing Thee Song of Araby*, the Russian dance, and the skating song. Following the Creole love song, Nettie and the girls marched up to the stage to receive their diplomas, and were graduates at last. After receiving their diplomas, the girls returned to their seats to sing *America*. After the recessional began, most likely *Pomp and Circumstance* played as the girls marched out of the auditorium.

It was a custom at the time for the graduating girls to be presented with a bouquet of flowers on graduation day, but since flowers were not allowed in the auditorium, Nettie's flowers awaited her on her desk in Miss Keenan's 8B classroom. On Nettie's desk must have sat a bouquet of red roses, surrounded by carnations, on a sheaf of ferns. Up in the classroom too waited her report card and autograph book. In her graduation portrait, Nettie is smiling, holding her diploma in one hand and her bouquet of flowers in the other. Although it is not known who in her family attended her graduation or who presented her with the flowers, her portrait proves that she received them.

Nettie on her graduation day from Public School 132 in 1929.
Notice she is wearing the dress she created during her sewing class.

While Nettie's diploma is long gone, and her graduating class photo vanished after her death, one item from eighth grade has survived the last seventy-five years, the autograph book.

Between the crumbling, golden covers of Nettie's eighth grade autograph book are the final testament to her grammar school years. In blue ink, Nettie wrote her class cheer as: "Little fishes in the book/Papa caught them with a hook/Mama fried them with a pan/Papa eats them like a man."

On the pastel colored pages of the autograph book are "forever pressed" the names and well wishes from her sister graduates, as well as dozens of "for-get-me-nots." Unlike today, the students went through half year school years, instead of full year school years. They had sixteen classes to pass instead of eight in grammar school. That is the explanation of Nancy Colucci's note to Nettie on a yellow colored page:

To Antoinette,

Sixteen classes you have passed.

Graduation here at last.

Other notes gave Nettie advice for the future:

To Nettie,

Needles to needles

Pins to pins

When you get married your troubles begin.

Your cousin,

Anna DiCandia

To Antoinette,

When you are old and cannot see pick up your glasses and think of me.

Your friend,

Graduate Loretta Rabito

To Nettie,

When you are married and have about (9) nine, bundle them up and come see mine.

A friend,

Margaret

To Nettie,

When you are married and your husband gets cross, pick up the broomstick and say "I'm the boss."

Your friend,

Lucy DiNapoli

To Nettie,

First comes love and then comes marriage. Then comes Nettie with the baby carriage.

From,

Cousin Agnes C(arrano)

Following Nettie's graduation from Public School 132, she enrolled at Eastern District High School. She only remained there for a short time and opted for continuation school in Williamsburg instead. She attended there for one night every week until she reached the age of sixteen. In finishing school, Nettie learned domestic skills, an extension to the cooking and sewing classes she had taken at 132.

After leaving school, Nettie, like her older brothers and sisters before her, entered the work force. Her expert sewing talents that she mastered from early childhood helped her land her first job at the Bilt-Rite Baby Carriage Factory at 1039 Metropolitan Avenue in Williamsburg.

"It was a very big building. A whole block long," Nettie's forelady and friend, Katie Riceputo said in 2001. Inside the large facility was a vast array of departments. "We had the upholsterers who used to upholster the inside of the carriage, the cutters, the hood sewers, and the wheel makers. And we had the carpenters who used to put the frames together. It was a very big place. I used to tell the girls what to do," Katie said.

The employees at Bilt-Rite worked eight hours a day, six days a week. "We worked steady. We never had a day off. Saturdays we always worked overtime." Katie said. "I was very important to [the bosses]. Nettie was very important to them, too. We became good [sewing machine] operators. Naturally, the bosses, Specter and Harrison, liked us. There were over a hundred people working there."

Nettie began her career shortly before the age of fifteen stuffing cushions for the carriages, bringing home a meager nine dollars a week. Before too long, she was promoted to sewing machine operator, alongside Katie Riceputo, and their friend, Inez. They sewed the carriage hoods on the sewing machines. "Nettie was my best girlfriend there and we became good friends and were always together, together with Inez." Katie said.

Nettie had lunch with her newfound friends, Katie and Inez, every day. "We always had lunch together," Katie said. "On Fridays, the three of us would go across the street to the lunch wagon for fishcakes and coffee without sugar. Inez put us on that diet of coffee without sugar and I still take coffee without sugar because of it."

Nettie in 1937

Back on the home front, while it was Connie who was dubbed the "Belle of Beadel Street" by "the young fellas who hung out in front of Dukey's candy store," Connie claimed it was Nettie who had a string of beaux enamored with her. Childhood chum Anthony

Lanzetta had been smitten with Nettie ever since childhood. Their families became forever entwined in 1932 when Anthony's sister, Sally, married Nettie's brother, Jimmy. Nettie had been a bride's maid and Anthony had been partnered with her as an usher. Anthony hoped that the union of their siblings would bring him closer to Nettie, but she was in love with someone else.

Jimmy and Sally Carrano and their wedding party in 1932.
Notice Nettie on the far left of the picture. Anthony Lanzetta is standing to her right.

"Nettie was going with this fella, Al," Connie remembered. Al's sister, Cecilia, was one of Nettie's closest friends. In fact, as the relationship between Nettie and Al seemed to grow more serious, Cecilia asked Nettie to stand godmother to her son when he was baptized. Cecilia believed that one day in the near future, Nettie would become her sister-in-law.

One person who was staunchly against Nettie's union with her Irish admirer was her father, Cono. Nettie and Cono had gotten into an argument about Al, which led him to strike Nettie across the face, a practice he had never had with his daughters. "My father had a little bit of resentment [against Nettie's relationship with Al] and Nettie got a slap once," Connie said.

Inside the front cover of Nettie's Public School 132 autograph book, Al wrote to Nettie:

To Nettie Carrano,
If someone loves you more than I, tell them to write in front of mine.

Al

Then in a heart he wrote: "To Nettie I love you From Al." He then proceeded to repeat this inscription on the first seven pages of the book.

Shortly after Nettie's argument with her father, she started having problems with Al and they broke up. While Cecilia was sobbing over losing Nettie as a possible sister-in-law, Anthony Lanzetta was beaming over the news and jumped at the opportunity to express his true feelings for Nettie. Just as the news of Nettie and Al's break-up spread, the doorbell rang at Kingsland Avenue and Nettie received a dozen long stemmed roses from Anthony.

"[Anthony] always liked Nettie," his sister, Sally, said. "He didn't go out with no other girls."

Shortly after Nettie broke off her relationship with Al, Anthony got an attack of his appendix. When Nettie received the news, she rushed to his bedside to visit the boy she called "lovey dovey" in his 1928 eighth grade autograph book. "[Anthony] loved Nettie for a long time," his brother, Nick, said. "When he got better, they started going out. They liked each other when they were kids. One time they took me and Connie with them on a double date. I imagine he liked Nettie his whole life."

Not long after they started dating, Nettie and Anthony were engaged. The couple began making plans for a November wedding and Sally began work on creating Nettie's wedding gown.

In the meantime, the Carranos were forced by the City of New York to leave their beloved home of 101 Beadel Street. The city decided they wanted to widen Vandervoot Avenue and would have to tear down some houses to accomplish this project. "They said they were going to throw down fourteen houses and our house was included," Connie said. "My father and the landlords of these other houses were forced to sell their homes because the city was taking over to build a wider street, and we were forced to move."

Brokenhearted, the Carranos left their home and moved into temporary housing in an apartment on North Henry Street, until Cono found a new house for them to live in. "For five months my father rented a house on North Henry Street in Greenpoint and in the meantime he was looking for a place," Connie said. "He wasn't used to paying rent to a landlord. So then he found a house on Kingsland Avenue."

A few blocks from the tenement house where Nettie was born, Cono bought 145 Kingsland Avenue, a two family attached brownstone four houses in from Meeker Avenue, in February of 1935. While Cono rented the top floor apartment to the Cotignola family, (it is unknown if they were any relation to Cono's mother, Rosa Cotignola Carrano), Cono and Maria moved into the first floor apartment with their unmarried children: Pat, Rosie, Anna, Nettie, Connie, Rocky, and Johnny.

Wedding bells were ready to ring for Nettie and Anthony in the fall of 1937, but Cono was less than pleased about this union of Nettie's also. "My father said [to Nettie] 'You marry him, you're going to be a young widow,'" Connie said. Cono did not approve of Anthony's precarious line of work, fireworks. He only saw disaster in Anthony's future.

The third of four children of Angelo (Anthony) and Mary (Stabulas) Lanzetta, Anthony was born Angelo Lanzetta on September 23, 1913, in Brooklyn, New York. Anthony had known Nettie from before her third birthday, when they lived on the second floor of 60 Kingsland Avenue. It was from early childhood that Anthony was drawn like a magnet to Nettie, and his sister, Sally, was equally drawn to Nettie's brother, Jimmy. The Lanzetta family moved frequently, leaving 60 Kingsland Avenue after six years. Besides owning his own firework business, based on Long Island, Anthony Sr. was also a barber by trade. It was this trade that led the

Lanzettas to move from one home to another. "Whenever my father got a job [as a barber], instead of taking transportation to work, we moved," Nick Lanzetta said.

After Nettie's brother, Frank and his wife were divorced in August of 1931, the Lanzettas took over their apartment on Beadel Street and once again lived with the Carranos. "We lived there for a couple of years, and then moved to Glendale," Nick said.

No matter how frequently the Lanzettas moved, the Carranos and Lanzettas never separated. Nettie's sister, Anna, followed the Lanzettas and visited them wherever they moved, since Sally was her best friend. Then when Jimmy and Sally married in November of 1932, the two families were united, as they were to be once again with the marriage of Nettie and Anthony.

Nettie was not deterred by her father's warning, and on November 7, 1937, the church bells of Saint Cecilia's rang for her. Dressed in Sally's original creation of silk chiffon velvet with white satin fan pleats in the front, and a veil ten yards long, Nettie walked down the aisle of Saint Cecilia's on her father's arm, as he reluctantly gave her away to her lifelong admirer. Father Eugene McGoughlin presided over the wedding, and in the presence of their witnesses, Nick Lanzetta and Concetta (Connie) Carrano, the childhood chums were pronounced man and wife.

Nettie and Anthony Lanzetta on their wedding day in 1937

Following the ceremony was a reception in Maspeth, Queens at the Clinton Hall.

"We had sandwich weddings back then," Sally laughed. "We all made the sandwiches. And they would bring out the trays of sandwiches. Kids would grab them and make them fall on the floor."

"I was in the band," Nick said. "I played for my brother's wedding. We had a good time."

Following the wedding, Nettie and Anthony moved to 215 Maujer Street in Williamsburg. "The apartment was furnished by my father," Nick said. "It was a very nice apartment. My Aunt Josie Carl lived in the same building and Cousin Sally Damiani lived next door. Rocky [Nettie's brother] was my best friend. Me and Rocky and my cousin Ralph Carl would go over there and play pinochle. We would buy buns and go over there for coffee. My brother and I were pretty close."

By 1937, Jimmy and Sally's marriage had gone sour and their battles pulled both families into their ongoing war. "Uncle Jimmy and Aunt Sally were steadily fighting," Nettie's son, Anthony Lanzetta Jr. said. "Their marriage was one big joke with sad endings after each battle." During these battles, Nettie and Anthony each defended their sibling, causing nasty rows between the two newlyweds. Another factor that caused Nettie a great deal of grief in her new marriage was that she was the breadwinner of the household. "Nettie was working at Bilt-Rite Baby Carriages," Nick Lanzetta said. "My brother only worked seasonal [during the firework season]. I don't think he had a job in the winter." Even during the firework season when Anthony worked for his father, his receipt of taking home wages was far and few between. Nettie was holding the household together single-handedly.

"I met Anthony," Katie Riceputo said. "He was a little bit of a thing. He looked like his sister, Sally. Nettie used to tell me he was a lazy thing and that she was so unhappy. She didn't know what she was going to do. He didn't support her. He never had any energy to support her. He was always on the island with the fireworks."

During the week in firework season, Anthony worked on Long Island at the firework factories in Haggerman with his father and brother, Nick. Anthony would pick Nettie up on Friday afternoons when she got off work to spend the weekends at the bungalow near the firework shop. During the summer of 1938, Nettie became pregnant with their first child. Unfortunately, in spite of her delicate condition, Nettie was unable to cut back on her workload. "Nettie worked until she almost gave birth at the plant," Connie said. "She was forced to work. Nettie didn't have such an easy life."

On Good Friday, April 7, 1939, Nettie gave birth to her first child. The baby was a son, named Anthony Lanzetta, after his father and grandfather. She gave birth at Saint Catherine's Hospital, not far away from her mother's home. At the Catholic hospital, Nettie was administered to by nuns, who were the nurses at the maternity facility. On April twenty third, Anthony was baptized at Saint Cecilia's. His godparents were the witnesses at his parents' wedding, his Uncle Nick and his Aunt Connie.

Nettie holding her newborn baby, Anthony on May 7, 1939 with her husband, Anthony to her right, and her brother, Rocky on her left. Her sister, Rosie is standing in the window.

A month after the christening, it was Memorial Day weekend. On Friday, May 26, 1939, Anthony and Nicky, along with their father, were working on firework displays in the factory in preparation for the weekend's festivities. Their mother, Mary, was also out there relaxing in the bungalow on the property. Later on in the afternoon, Anthony planned on driving to Brooklyn with Nicky to pick up

Nettie and Anthony to spend the weekend with him in Bellport. Nick Lanzetta remembered the events of this day in February 2003, at the age of eighty five:

"We used to go to Bellport and we would stay all week, from Monday to Friday. Then Friday afternoon, my brother and I would go in the car and we would go back to Brooklyn. He would pick up Nettie and Anthony and he would take them to Bellport and I would stay in Brooklyn to go play music or do whatever I was going to do. So that was a steady routine. This particular day, it was close to three o'clock. I was working in one building. Me and Anthony were working in one building together, and he finished his part of the job and said 'Nick, I'm gonna go tell Pop I'm all done. I say we'll get a good start and go to Brooklyn.' I said 'I've got about five more minutes work and I'll be done.' I was making the candles that go on the flags [type of firework]. So when my brother left the building I was in and he walked towards the chemical room, when he left that door, was the last I'd seen of him. Then, all of the sudden, I heard a big blast. When I ran out, I was hysterical. The whole shop was off the ground. There was nothing on the ground. Everything was up in the air. Metal, beams, you name it. And then I saw my father, where he was sitting was where I found him. He was all charred. It was not even half of his body. My brother got blown. When he got to that shop, the explosion came out the doors and he was near the door and he got blown, maybe one hundred feet away.

"My mother was in the bungalow, and a stick went through the house. My mother woke up and was hysterical. I ran out and she said 'Your brother! Your brother!' And I see him walking with all his clothes burnt off, and his hands, from putting the fire out, were hanging off like gloves. I picked him up and put him in the car. I didn't know where to touch him because he was burnt.

"When I picked him up and put him in the car, he said, 'Please God, don't let me die. Who is going to take care of my baby?' He had all his marbles, even with the concussion.

"Then other people came and took him to this nursing home. There was no hospital there. That is where they sedated him and stuff like that. My father got killed instantly. He never knew what hit him."

At the time of the accident, Nettie was finishing her day at work at Bilt-Rite. After she got off from work, she headed for her mother's house to get ready and wait for Anthony to pick her and the baby up for the weekend. Connie was with Nettie while she waited:

"Nettie was getting ready. She went every Friday to spend the weekend with her husband. She got the call at my mother's house. It was a terrible day. It was black Friday."

Anthony's two sisters, Rose Patanjo and Sally Carrano were also in Brooklyn at the time of the accident. According to Sally, Rose Patanjo's husband, Jim, was notified of the accident, and he brought the two sisters to the scene of the accident on Long Island. While Nick Lanzetta claims that Jim Patanjo drove Nettie to Long Island that afternoon, Sally says that due to another battle between her and her husband, which Nettie and Anthony had gotten dragged into, she and Nettie were not speaking to one another at the time of the accident. "Nettie and I were not on good terms on the day of the accident," Sally said.

The latest fight had ended with Jimmy Carrano punching Anthony in the face, leaving Nettie furious that her home had to be upset because of her brother and sister-in-law's unhappiness. Now her husband was bearing the bruise because of it, which only drove Nettie and Anthony further apart.

Therefore, it is uncertain how Nettie made the trip from Greenpoint to Patchogue, where Anthony, covered in second and third degree burns over his entire body, was being treated for his injuries at a nursing facility. While Sally and Rose had made the trip to Long Island also, only Nettie was allowed to see Anthony that night.

"I was there when Nettie walked in," Nick said, "and [Anthony] recognized her. He said 'hello, honey' or something like that."

Nettie was frightened at the sight of his face, blackened from the burns, and his head very large from the swelling. "He kept saying, 'my baby, my baby.' He was worried about the baby," Connie said. "Anthony was only six weeks old when that happened."

After Nettie saw Anthony, they all left and went back home to Brooklyn. "I didn't think he was going to die," Nick said. Nettie said she never would have left that night if she thought that Anthony would die.

Shortly after midnight on May twenty seventh, Anthony died from internal injuries due to the accident.

"Nettie took it bad," Katie Riceputo said. "She took it terrible. She couldn't get over it. Her family helped her through it."

Anthony Sr. and Jr. were returned to Greenpoint for their wake and funeral. "Anthony and my father were laid out at 551 Graham Avenue," Nick said. "There was glass on top of Anthony's coffin. It was sealed. My father's was closed. It was a ninety five degree heat wave and they were laid out for five days. I remember the undertaker used to come and spray stuff in the morning [for the stench]." With summer just around the corner, the four room railroad flat became stifling, as people crammed into the small rooms to pay their respects, as the temperature continued to rise.

"The whole neighborhood came to see father and son laid out on Graham Avenue in the mother's rooms," Connie said. "Mobs came to see them. It was a sad experience for everyone, knowing Nettie was left with a six week old baby."

Rose Zambrotta Carrano, who would become Nettie's sister-in-law in 1942, when she married Rocky Carrano, remembered going to the wake with her sister-in-law, Aggie, who was Nettie's cousin. Nettie had been the maid-of-honor when Aggie married Rose's brother, Nick, in 1937. "Aggie loved Nettie very much. How Aggie cried! 'My cousin Nettie lost her husband!' I went to the wake with Aggie. She told me about it and I went with her. I didn't know Nettie well then, but I had met her. It was in the house and there were two caskets. A lot of people went out of curiosity too. It was terrible."

Nettie's friend, Katie Riceputo, remembered when she went to pay her respects, "the smell was terrible from the burnt bodies. The grandmother [Mary Lanzetta] wanted to see the [body of] the grandfather [Anthony Sr.] and the stink that came out of the coffin! I can't imagine what she saw in there. Anthony had glass over his coffin."

"My mother never should have opened that casket," Nick said.

On May thirty first, following their funeral mass at Saint Francis de Paola Church, Anthony Sr. and Jr. were laid to rest in Saint John's Cemetery, the same place where Carmela and Mama Rosa were buried the decade before.

"My mother got a plot in St. John's cemetery for nine burials," Nick said. "She bought the plots, the stone and expensive caskets. She had insurance on [her husband and son]. She had double indemnity for accidental death."

Following Anthony's death, Nettie was left a "penniless" widow, to use her own word, with an infant son. "[Nettie] didn't receive a dime," Connie said. "Her mother-in-law got double indemnity and Nettie didn't even get a dime."

"My mother could have done a lot more for Nettie," Nick said. "She should have helped Nettie out. Nettie went back to work at the carriage place after a while. I had to go to work to support my mother."

After the shock of the tragedy had passed, Nettie had to make arrangements to return to work and have someone take care of Anthony during the day. She decided to leave her apartment on Maujer Street in August and asked the landlord to give her rooms to her sister, Connie, who would be getting married that month. Leaving Maujer Street, Nettie took an apartment two doors away from 60 Kingsland Avenue, where she was born, in the building formerly owned by the Gordon family, her childhood friends. They had moved to Kings Highway many years before, but to the Carranos, that building would always be "The Gordons." Still living at 60 Kingsland Avenue were Nettie's aunt and uncle, Maria and Giuseppe Focarile, as well as many of their children. Their son, Charlie, had died only fifteen days before Anthony, and his widow, Mary, was willing to baby-sit for Anthony while Nettie worked. Also, to help Nettie in her new apartment, her sister, Rosie, came to live with her there. With all of her arrangements set, Nettie was able to return to her old job at Bilt-Rite.

"[Nettie] had it hard," her sister-in-law, Rose Carrano said. "I don't think people realized how hard she had it."

Nettie standing at her husband's grave in August 1939

While some may have crumbled under Nettie's circumstances, she refused to let herself be vanquished. In August of 1939, when the Lanzetta headstone was placed on the grave in St. John's Cemetery, a photograph was taken of Nettie standing behind it. Clad in a wide-brimmed black mourning bonnet and black dress, according to the customs of Italy and Brooklyn, she looked straight into the camera, arms folded and resting on the stone, with determination of tempered steel. Her eyes are direct and seem to say that she has suffered a great deal, but she will carry on. A much often quoted line attributed to the late first lady Jacqueline Kennedy Onassis shortly before her death in 1994 seems a fitting caption for this photo:

"I have been through a lot and have suffered a great deal. But I have had lots of happy moments, as well. Every moment one lives is different from the other. The good, the bad, hardship, the joy,

the tragedy, love, and happiness are all interwoven into one single, indescribable whole that is called life. You cannot separate the good from the bad. And perhaps there is no need to do so, either."

According to Sally, Nettie needed to undergo an emotional convalescence following the tragedy and retreated to the Carranos to regain her strength. While Sally and Nettie mourned the loss of the same man, the rift that had taken place shortly before the tragedy would only grow in the following decades. "Nettie stayed with her family and I stayed with mine," Sally said.

Wearing her widow's weaves, Nettie proudly holds her infant son up for all the world to see in August 1939

Nettie had a reason to go on. The same week that she had her picture taken at her husband's grave, someone had taken a picture of her, dressed in her black dress, black stockings, and black shoes, standing in the backyard of her mother's home, a radiant smile beaming from her face as she holds her infant son above her head towards the sky for all the world to see. If for nothing else, she would go on for him.

"Nettie survived," Connie said. "[The Carranos were] a large family and you could expect things to happen, and they did."

CHAPTER FOUR

WIDOW
1939 – 1949

The year 1939 was a year that defined Nettie for the rest of her life. It was the year she became a mother. It was the year she became a widow. It was this year she was hardened by tragedy and strengthened by struggle. She learned how to fight for survival; not only for herself, but for her infant child. During the year that she would reflect on constantly over the next fifty years, she would remember seeing the impossible made possible during the summer of 1939 in Flushing Meadow at the World's Fair. Then, as the year that her life was irrevocably changed drew to a close, she was introduced to the screen heroine she would relate to and would remain an icon for her for the rest of her days.

In the midst of Nettie's tragedy, Connie married Tony Rizza on August 6, 1939, at Saint Cecilia's. Nettie was supposed to be Connie's matron-of-honor, but due to the circumstances of the tragedy, their sister, Rosie, stood maid-of-honor. "Anthony died in May and I got married in August," Connie said. "[The wedding reception] was held at Kingsland Avenue. With Nettie being in mourning, we didn't want to have a big wedding."

Connie and Tony settled into Nettie's old apartment on Maujer Street, as she, along with Rosie and Anthony, settled into their new home on Kingsland Avenue. Nettie returned to work at Bilt-Rite, Rosie worked as a sewing machine operator at the Brooklyn Navy Yard, and Anthony was taken care of by Mary Focarile, until Nettie returned from work after the five o'clock whistle blew.

While there were very few diversions from the tragedy for Nettie for the remainder of 1939, two events left indelible marks on her for the rest of her life, the 1939-1940 World's Fair and the release of the film, *Gone with the Wind* on December 15, 1939.

John Crowley described the essence of the magic of the World's Fair that swept Nettie away in the documentary film, *The World of Tomorrow*. "I think that there are moments where you can see the world turning from what it is into what it will be. For me, the New York World's Fair is such a moment. It is a compass rose pointing in all directions, toward imaginary future and real past, false future and immutable present, a world of tomorrow contained in the lost American yesterday."

Just as Nettie became a mother, the World's Fair opened in Flushing Meadow in April 1939 with the motto "Building a World for Tomorrow." The different exhibits at the World's Fair showed that the key to freedom and prosperity was the new age of science and technology. Much like the "Land of Oz" in the film *The Wizard of Oz* that premiered on August 18, 1939, the World's Fair was a vibrant world that gave all who visited its grounds hope for the future.

The Fair was opened by President Franklin Delano Roosevelt on April 30, 1939, when he revealed the greatest technological advance that would change society as it was known up until that point forever, the new age of television. That was the day that New York City had its first public broadcasting. Coming ten years after the stock market crash and two years before the United States entered World War II, it seemed hopeful that the World's Fair would impact the depression era the same way the Renaissance Age brought light to the medieval Dark Ages in Europe. While the World's Fair did bring hope to the masses, the reality of this new era being ushered in seemed uncertain, as the outbreak of war seemed imminent in Europe.

When the World's Fair closed on Halloween 1939, war had erupted in Europe the month before. When the Fair reopened after the winter season on May 11, 1940, the optimistic hope of the new age was impacted by the harsh reality of war. Admission was reduced from seventy-five cents to fifty cents for adults. The Soviet Pavilion was replaced by the "American Common." Fountain Lake in the amusements area had been renamed Liberty Lake. The British, Polish, Czechoslovakian, and Finnish exhibits all reflected their entry into the war. By the time the World's Fair closed for the last time on October 27, 1940, the focus of the new technological age that was going to be ushered in by the 1960s had been lost, as the new focus became the war raging in Europe and the possibility of the United States entering the war became more likely.

During the summer of 1939, the war in Europe was as far from Nettie's mind as it was in miles around the globe. She was fighting her own battle for survival and reinventing herself as a widowed, working mother trying to make ends meet and come out on top. Nettie did not think about having good times or carefree days. Either she was at work or caring for her infant son. The focus of her life and her reason for living became her baby. On rare occasions, when she got a babysitter for Anthony, Nettie, dressed in full mourning garb, would join Connie for the nickel subway ride and seventy-five cents admission to the park, and take in the exhibits that seemed to her amazingly unbelievable and impossible. As the daughter of a woman who over forty years before had washed her clothes with rocks in the river, she was seeing advances like a box that would be in your living room that would show movies and shows like you went to see in the movie houses. It was inconceivable. Only twelve years before, she had been going to see films that were black and white and silent. Now they were in color and had sound. It was amazing to think that the new technology would bring this right into your home. As Nettie walked through the gate, she left the sad state of her life today at the gate, as she explored the possibilities and wonders of the World of Tomorrow.

In the fall and winter of 1939, Connie was ecstatic over the upcoming release of the film adaptation of the 1,037 page novel she had read the year before, *Gone with the Wind* by Margaret Mitchell. She had envisioned different actors for the many roles in the film and even sent in ballots to movie magazines with her choices for the roles. There was a world-wide search for the actress who would play the film's heroine, Scarlett O'Hara. After testing nearly every female actress around, the director David O. Selznick met a virtually unknown twenty five-year-old British actress, Vivien Leigh, who would come to personify the role and become an icon of the world for all-time.

Gone with the Wind, starring Vivien Leigh and Clark Gable (Nettie's all-time favorite actor) in the title roles, premiered in Atlanta on December 15, 1939. Shortly after the film's premier, Nettie joined Connie and her new husband, Tony, and waited in line for hours in Manhattan to see the nearly four hour film epic. While Connie had always been the reader and writer of the family, Nettie had never been a reader, so as the lights dimmed in the movie house, and Max Steiner's score blasted through the theater, and the wind-swept letters sailed across the screen, the story of the Civil War saga was totally foreign to Nettie. Nettie could not relate to the excitement and anticipation that had overtaken Connie, nor could she have been prepared for the impact the next few hours would have on the rest of her life.

Over the next four hours, which included an intermission, Nettie was captivated and awestruck, to put it mildly. For the first time in her life, Nettie had found a heroine she could relate to and identify with, through her many trials and tribulations. She watched with amazement as she saw a woman experience many of the obstacles she had to overcome in the past year and do so victoriously. Over the next five decades, as her life experiences grew, Nettie would find more in common with this heroine, Scarlett O'Hara, as she matured and entered old age. She saw the young, carefree girl surrounded by beaux become a young widow. Nettie, herself, was still wearing her widow's weaves at this time, now seven months after her husband's death. It struck a chord in Nettie to see another young widow like herself and all of the emotional turmoil that accompanies the experience. Equally as poignant for Nettie, she saw this woman struggle and fight to survive nearly crushing blows, suffering the pains of hell and rising from the ashes, when she stands in an open field at dawn, penniless, holds her head erect and shakes her fist at the sky saying "As God is my witness; they are not going to lick me." This scene is reminiscent of that photograph of Nettie at the grave of her dead, young husband and the one of her holding her infant son towards the sky with the ebullient smile on her face that August. Scarlett O'Hara Hamilton was not going to be licked. Neither was Nettie Carrano Lanzetta.

As Nettie left the Manhattan movie house that December night, "Tara's Theme" would forever become a haunting and welcomed reminder of a youth tempered by tragedy. Rhett Butler tells Scarlett in the film, they have witnessed a historic moment that she could tell her grandchildren one day how she saw the Old South disappear one night. Nearly forty-nine years after that night, Nettie would be telling her grandson about the historic moment when the film *Gone with the Wind* changed her life. Nettie's Tara would become 145 Kingsland Avenue, the home she spent her life trying to protect and preserve; no matter where else she may live in her life or how long she lived.

As the decade of the 1930s drew to a close and the 1940s were ushered in, Nettie, at the age of twenty five, was coming to terms with her new role as widow and working mother.

"I always felt sorry for Nettie and she had Anthony," sister-in-law, Rose Carrano said. "Anthony looked just like Mickey Rooney. I used to feel sorry that he had no daddy. Nettie had to work and leave the kid with this lady, Mary, who used to mind him. It was sad. Very sad. It was not easy for her to go to work and leave the baby. I don't think she ever dated. She probably had a lot of opportunities."

Compounded with being a single working mother, a constant cross that Nettie had to bear was Anthony's constant illnesses. "She had a lot of trouble when Anthony was small," Katie Riceputo said. "He was always sick. She didn't go out much. She had her son. [Nettie] never had no good times at all. She was always crying. She had so much hard luck. She felt God didn't love her. [Anthony] had scarlet fever. He was always sick."

More than two years after war erupted in Europe, the Japanese led a surprise attack bombing on Pearl Harbor at 7:53 A.M. on Sunday, December 7, 1941. In the wake of the Japanese attack, 2,403 American military were killed, 188 destroyed planes, and a crippled Pacific fleet that included eight damaged or destroyed battleships, most notably, the USS Arizona, which rests in its watery tomb at the bottom of the Pacific Ocean for the past sixty three years.

Over the airwaves the next day, President Franklin Delano Roosevelt addressed Congress, and the world, saying "Yesterday, December 7, 1941 – a date which will live in infamy – the United States of America was suddenly and deliberately attacked by naval and air forces of the Empire of Japan … As commander in chief of the Army and Navy, I have directed that all measures be taken for our defense … No matter how long it may take us to overcome this premeditated invasion, the American people in their righteous might will win through to absolute victory … I ask that the Congress declare that since the unprovoked and dastardly attack by Japan on Sunday, December 7, a state of war has existed between the United States and the Japanese empire."

Following Roosevelt's speech, the United States entered World War II, and the Carranos were off to Europe.

As Scarlett O'Hara had seen when the Civil War broke out in *Gone with the Wind*, Nettie saw most of the young men of Greenpoint enlisting in the different branches of the military. Many of her childhood friends and former beaux left for Europe, some never to return. Of Nettie's six brothers, two would be enlisted to fight for "democracy."

Nettie's mother, Maria (center), surrounded by six of her ten living children, including Nettie standing at right, and two of her seven grandchildren during World War II in 1943

"The war years as I recall were a bad time for everyone," Nettie's son, Anthony remembers. "Uncle John was enlisted and went away to England. Uncle Pat was called up, even though he was in his forties. As soon as Uncle John left for service, Mom and I moved from Gordon's rooms on Kingsland Avenue to 145 Kingsland Avenue."

"Then Nettie had to break up her home," sister-in-law Rose remembers around 1942. "[Nettie] moved back to Kingsland Avenue. She had it hard. I don't think people realized how hard she had it." Once there was enough room at 145 Kingsland Avenue, Cono went to see Nettie and told her to come home. She would not have to pay rent and she would no longer have to worry about Anthony while she was at work.

"Aunt Anna, Mom, and I slept in one room," Anthony said. "Aunt Rosie slept in the living room. Uncle Pat and Uncle Johnny slept in the room upstairs without heat. By that time, Uncle Rocky, Aunt Connie, Uncle Jimmy, Uncle Mikey, and Uncle Frankie were gone already. Mom was working at Bilt-Rite Baby Carriage Company and would drop me off at Mary Focarile's on her way to work every morning. Mom had to support me, so her days with me were limited. Grandma [Maria Carrano] was her substitute. So was Aunt Rosie.

"When Mom and I moved to 145 Kingsland Avenue, Grandma Carrano was still cooking and going to mass every morning, returning with bagels and rolls from Angelo's store on the corner. Grandma was the person that kept our family together all those years. She generated a very special kind of love, like a magnet. Her biggest cross was Grandpa Carrano getting drunk and causing trouble, so she made sure everyone stayed clear of him."

"I can remember the nights during the war. At night, we had blackouts. All the lights would be turned off and the blinds closed. You could hear all the air raids sirens screaming into the night. I can also remember getting food stamps and rations. You could only get a certain amount of articles and food. Some items I remember mostly were gas, butter, cigarettes, milk, some clothes, and meats. Grandma [Carrano] would buy most of her meats at George's and Trunz. Chicken she got at the chicken market on Beadel Street."

While Nettie may not have had any time for love at this time in her life, there was one man who was very much in love with her, and he was only one door away. John Russo, Nettie's next-door neighbor, of 143 Kingsland Avenue was smitten with Nettie and made his affections known to her. "She really liked John Russo and he probably really cared for her too," Nettie's sister-in-law, Rose said. "She was really attractive." John went as far as to tell Nettie that he wanted to marry her, but with the war going on, Nettie feared becoming a widow once again. John was drafted into the army and was stationed in California, before he was sent overseas. On January 26, 1943, John sent Nettie a lace trimmed powder blue handkerchief with a poem printed on it:

For-get-me not
When the golden
Sun is sinking
And your mind
From troubles free

Nettie

When of others you

Are thinking

Will you sometimes think of me?

Shortly after John sent the handkerchief to Nettie, he was shipped overseas, where he was killed in combat. Nettie saved that handkerchief in the envelope she received it in for the rest of her life.

Following the death of John Russo, his brother, Pat, had a son he named after his late brother. Pat asked Nettie to stand godmother to the newborn John Russo.

On V - E Day, Kingsland Avenue celebrated and Nettie wept and rejoiced. On V - J Day, Kingsland Avenue celebrated and was decorated, and Nettie wept and rejoiced once again. "My mother was very proud of being an American and being a New Yorker," said Nettie's daughter, Ann Marie Franzese. "According to her, there is no place like New York and no one 'does it' like New York."

"I can remember the big fireworks and parties," Anthony said. "It was really a time to celebrate." John returned safely home from England, much to the relief of the family. Pat served as a medic and was never sent overseas. He too returned safely home to Kingsland Avenue. On reflection of his tour in the military, Pat composed a poem that he would recite at family gatherings over the decades to come:

Twas twilight on the desert

Peter M. Franzese

The bugle has sounded retreat
A soldier returns from his battle
To rest his aching feet
He is dusty, tired, and bitter
For the wind, the sun, and the sand
Had scorch-burned and parched him
As he traveled on the land

He lays in his bunk thinking
Of his loved ones so far away
He longs to be home with them
To spend a pleasant day
He shuts his eyes in slumber
And dreams of home sweet home
Where there is no desert
But the fields in which he roams

On through the night he slumbers
As sound as he can be
To the moment he hears the bugle
To get up for forever leave
He has his chow and then places it
Where cigarette butts lay
He rolls his pack and off he goes
To the desert for another day

When his training is over
He'll be shipped across the sea
To die in the field of battle
To save democracy

When this war is over
The whole world will be gay
The sun will shine where the soldier died
On a foreign field far away

There shall be no more wars
We shall punish those to blame
The world shall have everlasting peace
The soldier shall never die again.

Through war and peace, Kingsland Avenue remained the headquarters and focal point of the Carrano family. "Lots of problems were solved there and some problems were caused there also," Anthony said. "Everyone was always at 145 Kingsland Avenue for some reason or another. It was still everyone's home."

The Cotignolas vacated the second floor apartment of 145 Kingsland Avenue and Frank moved in there with his wife, Millie, whom he married in 1934, and their two children, Lucille and Conrad. They would remain there until 1957.

While it seemed the stormy marriage of Jimmy and Sally could not affect Nettie's life to the magnitude it did during her eighteen-month-marriage to Anthony, their bitter battles took center stage many times on Kingsland Avenue. "Their marriage was one big joke with incidents after each battle," Anthony said. "Once incident was when Aunt Sally started a fight with the sisters [Nettie, Connie, Rosie, and Anna] and Mom and Aunt Sally tangled up. Aunt Sally bit Mom on the thumb and Mom required stitches. The fight was over marriage problems. It sure was a bad spectacle. It took years for Mom to recover from that incident."

Family traditions were created as more grandchildren came every few years. There were eight grandchildren in the Carrano family by the close of 1945. On every Friday, Maria would make a large pot of escarole, pasta e fagoli, and potato omelets. Most of the married sons would come home for dinner with the family. In the mid-1940s, Cono decided to finish off the basement and install a kitchen down there. Maria enjoyed her basement kitchen thoroughly and spent most of her day cooking down there. Due to the larger area, the family could celebrate holidays together, whereas it was very tight doing so in Maria and Cono's apartment.

"Now the whole family could gather for holidays," Anthony said, "and boy did we gather - not only for holidays, but every Sunday, and then some! I think the basement brought the family even closer together."

"Every Sunday was Mother's Day at my mother's house and we all gathered there," Connie said.

"Holidays were a special time for our family," Anthony said. "Grandma and Mom would start cooking early for the coming holidays like Christmas, which was the biggest. Zeppoles were at the top of the list. Grandma had her own recipe, but Mom modified it just a little."

While the basement was host to family gatherings during the winter months, Cono's Elmont bungalow where Nettie and her sisters passed the summers of their youth in the 1920s and 1930s now became the host to the next generation of Carrano children. "All the kids were sent out there for weeks at a time," Anthony said. "By the 1940s, the bungalow finally got electricity, an indoor toilet, and sink. Up until then, the outhouse, or "backhouse," as it was called, was the only bathroom facilities available."

Nettie with Anthony on his First Holy Communion day in 1946

By the mid-1940s, Anthony reached school age, so Nettie no longer needed to drop him off at Mary Focarile's home on her way to work. Instead, Maria got Anthony ready for school, which he began in kindergarten at Saint Cecilia's. In spite of the bad memories that Nettie and her sisters had at the school around 1920, Saint Cecilia's was attended by most of the Carrano grandchildren, and both church and school remain beloved and sacred places in both memory and family history.

On November 14, 1947, Maria and Cono celebrated their fiftieth wedding anniversary. The children held a celebration to mark the remarkable milestone down the basement of Kingsland Avenue. Around this time, Maria suffered a debilitating heart-attack that weakened her indomitable strength and ability to preside over her progeny. Maria was no longer able to be the pillar of strength that carried her family through the best and the worst of time, as her health deteriorated and her ability to single-handedly run the family ebbed away. Nettie had to continue working at Bilt-Rite, because she still had to support Anthony. Rosie continued to work until crippling arthritis forced her into retirement, for which she was unable to receive a pension for a matter of only months. Following her retirement, taking care of Maria as she declined became her full-time job. Cooking became Nettie's job. "Grandma slowly, but surely, recovered from the heart attack, but was not able to do what she used to do, but she managed to get along. Mom and Aunt Rosie were her crutches. The others helped as they could," Anthony said.

As the 1940s drew to a close, Anna married fourteen days before her thirty eighth birthday to Carmelo (Charlie) Abramo on April 10, 1948. Anna had gone out with Nettie and their niece, Marie, one night where they met Charlie and he bought them a pizza pie. He was the son of the undertaker, Domenico "Jim" Abramo, owner of Abramo Funeral Home on the corner of Humboldt Street and Skillman Avenue. Perhaps even more ironic, Charlie was the grandson of Pasqualina Abramo, the midwife who had delivered Nettie and Anna when they were born.

Nettie was still single, struggling, and working hard to make ends meet a decade after the tragedy in the spring of 1949. Besides the love affair Nettie almost had with John, she had not gone out with anyone throughout the 1940s. This is most likely because her time was so limited because of work and caring for her son. After a decade of this constant cycle, Nettie became used to never going anywhere and, according to Katie Riceputo, it was a chore to get Nettie to go anywhere for enjoyment. Still Nettie's dearest friend since they were teenagers, Katie coaxed Nettie into going out one Sunday in June of 1949 that would change the course of Nettie's life forever.

CHAPTER FIVE
AGAIN

1949 – 1959

It was a humid evening on Sunday, June 19, 1949, when Nettie's Bilt-Rite friend, Katie Riceputo insisted that she join her in celebrating her Aunt Helen's birthday at the Horseshoe Bar in Sunnyside. Nettie rarely went out in the ten years since she was widowed, due to the fact that she worked so much and she had a ten year old son at home, but Katie was insistent. After quite a bit of coaxing, and not wanting to disappoint Katie's Aunt Helen, of whom she was very fond, Nettie decided that even though she had work the next morning, she would go along.

That night, Katie and Helen picked Nettie up in a taxi at her home and the three ladies sat in the near empty bar and talked. The bartender was a neighbor of the Carranos from Kingsland Avenue, so Nettie had nothing to be concerned about. In fact, the only other people in the bar were two gentlemen on the opposite side of the room from them.

As the night wore on, the bartender came over to their table with drinks and a birthday cake for Helen. He said it was sent by one of the gentlemen from the other side of the room. Eventually, the young man who had generously sent over the cake and drinks made his way over to their table and introduced himself. His name was

Bob Boniface, and his buddy's name was Al Piecora. Following the introductions, Bob asked Nettie to dance with him.

As Bob danced with this beautiful stranger, he did not see the struggles and tragedies she had endured in her eyes. For those few, short minutes as he twirled her around the room, Nettie was able to forget about her heavy burdens, her sorrows, and her responsibilities. For the first time in ten years, Nettie was held in the arms of a man, and she was instantly swept off her feet by his charm.

After the dance was over, Nettie retreated to the bathroom with Katie and Helen to talk about her admirer. Thirty-four years later, Nettie gushed how the three of them thought they were two nice guys and the perfect gentlemen.

Later on in the evening, Bob offered to take the girls home in a taxi. He dropped off Nettie on Kingsland Avenue, Katie, then Helen. He and Nettie exchanged phone numbers, which she wrote in blue ink in the small, brown phone book she kept in her pocket book. Bob had mentioned to Nettie that he was going on vacation. As she left the taxi and walked up the front stoop of Kingsland Avenue, she must have felt like she was in a daze. For the first time in many, many years, Nettie was in love.

"She loved him so much," Katie Riceputo said fifty years later. "I made Nettie call him. She didn't want to call him because [Nettie thought] he was too young. I said to her to call him, what could you lose? I made her call him. I knew he was a wonderful guy. He liked her so much."

Not wanting to waste any time and determined to see her friend finally receive the happiness that had eluded her for so long, Katie pushed Nettie to call Bob before he left for his vacation. "When [Bob] found out [Nettie] liked him, he was so happy," Katie said.

While Bob was on vacation, he sent Nettie a postcard and told her that he missed her and wished she were there. Then, when he returned home, he picked up the phone and called her. When Bob set up his first date with Nettie, he still did not know that she was a widow, and a mother. For their first date, Bob brought Nettie to the Sunnyside Pool. Nettie recalled laughing in 1983 that Al had told her "you betta bring about ten sandwiches." Bob swore it was because Al was jealous of him. After their first date, everything went very rapidly, because they were engaged by the fall of 1949.

As Bob walked down Kingsland Avenue to meet Nettie's family for the first time, he was nearly run over by a ten year old boy on a bicycle. Much to his surprise, he was introduced to this little boy a little while later as Nettie's son! Bob was the first boyfriend that Nettie had since her husband's death, so it was somewhat difficult for her son to accept in the beginning.

"I had mixed emotions about the whole thing being ten and always having had Mom all to myself." Anthony said. The Carranos immediately embraced Bob into their fold and the Lanzettas gave their sincere blessing for a happy life for Nettie and Bob. "Bob was good to us," Nick Lanzetta said. "We were so glad [Nettie] got a good husband. She deserved it." After Bob because a fixture in the family, Anthony too came to accept that there would be another man in his mother's life. "I didn't have any problems accepting the whole thing after getting to know Bob," Anthony said.

On April 29, 1950, Nettie stood in her mother's bedroom and was surrounded by her sisters and sisters-in-law as she dressed to walk down the aisle of Saint Cecilia's for the second time in her life. Much had changed since she stood in this room and put on her white silk chiffon velvet gown twelve years before. She was not marrying out of duty or because of family pressure. She was also not marrying because she needed to be taken care of or because she had some silly notions in her head about a life after marriage. There wouldn't be much pomp and circumstance, just a quiet reception at home, with close relatives and friends. This time, Nettie was marrying simply for love. For the first time in her life, she had fallen deeply in love. Perhaps even more gratifying, the man that she was going to marry later that day was as deeply in love with her as she was with him.

Scores of relatives, friends, and onlookers filled the pews of Saint Cecilia's that day to see the tragic young widow, Nettie Carrano Lanzetta, finally remarry after nearly eleven years of widowhood. People young and old pushed against the edges of the pews down the center aisle of the church, and others lined the marble stairs and sidewalk, as Nettie made her way up the back staircase and down the aisle, dressed in a pink, low-cut gown, on the arm of her oldest brother, Frank Carrano. As she walked down the aisle this time, she had the widest smile that anyone had ever seen grace her face. She did not have the dread filling her heart as when her father told her that she would be a young widow. Instead, at the altar, Nettie saw the man she later described as her "knight in shining armor" waiting to become the husband she would have in good times and in bad, for better or worse, and in sickness and in health. For over a decade, Nettie had felt her life was over, but a popular tune that was being carried over the airwaves at the time captured the inner feelings of her heart, and would become the song that epitomized the day she married Bob Boniface, *Again*, because she never thought she would find happiness and love ever again.

Nettie got a second chance at happiness. She never thought that she would ever marry again, but here she was walking down the aisle, to Bob Boniface. As Al and Katie's daughter, Rose stood at their sides, Nettie and Bob were pronounced husband and wife by Father John J. Hannon.

Nettie and Bob Boniface on their wedding day in 1950

Following the ceremony, everyone returned to Kingsland Avenue, where the reception was held in the Carranos' basement, before Nettie and Bob were whisked away to Florida for their honeymoon.

Bob Boniface, the newest member to the Carrano clan, was born Angelo Robert Bonifacio on May 17, 1927, in Kings County Hospital, Brooklyn, New York. The third of four children of James and Innocenza Rose (Luppino) Boniface, Bob was raised in a multitude of Brooklyn neighborhoods, but lived mostly in the Ridgewood section of Brooklyn as a child. His family constantly moved and never really put down roots in one area. Bob came from a much younger and smaller family than the Carranos. His grandmother, Giuseppina Luppino, was Cono's age and his mother, Rose, was the age of Nettie's brother, Pat, so his parents were much more modern and Americanized than Nettie's.

Bob's father, James Boniface, born in 1892, was the son of a count in Locarno, Switzerland, who had also been a past mayor of Castellamare di Stabia, Italy, and an heir to the explorer who discovered the Straits of Bonifacio between Corsica and Sardinia. His mother, Innocenza (Rose), born in 1901, was the daughter of a macaroni manufacturer based in New Haven, Connecticut. Rose had been raised in Trapani, Sicily and Egypt. Along with her sister, Pia, Rose was raised in a convent in Trapani before her father came back to Italy to take the sisters to live in the United States in 1914.

James immigrated to the United States in 1918 and was an officer in the U.S. army, stationed in France during World War I.

Following the end of the war, with no place to call home, James went home with his friend, George Luppino and his wife, Helen, to New Haven, Connecticut, where George's father had the macaroni factory. It was there that James met George's sister, Rose, and they were married in 1920. When Rose's father died from a stroke in 1923, James, Rose, and their three year old daughter, Julia, once again uprooted and moved to Hoyt Street in the Carroll Gardens section of Brooklyn, where George Luppino had made his new home. The Bonifaces had lost an infant daughter, Gloria, a short time before. Four years after they returned to Brooklyn, Bob was born, followed by another son, Salvatore "Tuddie," in 1930. Bob had served in the U.S. Coast Guard at the tail end of World War II and he was working for the New York City Transit Authority when he married Nettie.

In spite of people's happiness for Nettie and Bob's newfound happiness, there was gossip that some did not believe their marriage would last, since Nettie and Bob had a nearly thirteen year age gap between them. Nettie was afraid of the gossip at first, but Katie had supported her and given her the courage to face the gossips. While Bob's parents were not opposed to the idea, his sister, Julia, was outraged over the age difference between Bob and Nettie. She fought vehemently with Bob, saying that he had no business marrying a woman so much older than he and with a child no less. Thirty-three years after their marriage, Bob and Nettie made a statement on home video to those people saying "this marriage wasn't supposed to last, but here we are after thirty-three years and we're still going strong!"

When Nettie and Bob returned from their Florida honeymoon, they moved with Anthony into an apartment in Greenpoint to be near Nettie's mother, Maria. They got an apartment in the home of Maria's dearest friend, Giuseppina Manzolillo, whom Nettie called "Cuma Peppina," because she had been a godmother in the Carrano family. In fact, "Cuma Peppina's" daughter, Mary, was married to one of Nettie's Carrano cousins also. Later in that year, Nettie became pregnant, but suffered a miscarriage. She would become pregnant again during the summer of 1951, and in the spring of 1952, she would give Bob his first child.

At 11:40 A.M. on April 23, 1952, Nettie gave birth to her first child in thirteen years at Carson C. Peck Memorial Medical Center in Brooklyn. She and Bob had a daughter, whom they named Ann Marie, after Saint Ann and her daughter, Mary, the Blessed Mother. Nettie and Bob were thrilled with their new baby with the cascade of black ringlets. Ann Marie was baptized at Saint Cecilia's- the setting of all the religious events in Nettie's life- on May 11, 1952, by Father Mooney. The godparents were the witnesses at their wedding, Al and Rose.

Nettie and Bob with Ann Marie in 1953

Following Ann Marie's birth, Nettie retired from Bilt-Rite, after working there for about twenty-three years. As a gift for Nettie's newborn Ann Marie, Bilt Rite gave Nettie a high chair and a carriage for her. Although she retired, she did return there for a few weeks when Ann Marie was small to fill in for her friend, Katie Riceputo. Her sister-in-law, Rosie, Rocky's wife, took care of Ann Marie for those few weeks while she worked. Nettie could never say no to a friend to whom she owed so much.

The year following Ann Marie's birth, 1953, was a monumental year, especially in Bob's life. Bob's father, James Boniface, died on the night of April 9th of a heart attack at his McKibben Street home. He was sixty one years of age. Nettie was especially crushed by his death because she had found a true friend in her new father-in-law, as opposed to her domineering mother-in-law, Rose, with whom she never saw eye-to-eye. Rose was very demanding of her sons, even after they were married and had families of their own. "Nana Boniface was a very over-powering mother-in-law," Nettie's daughter, Ann Marie said. "She had a very tumultuous relationship with my mother. My mother respected her because she was my father's mother, but she did not like her at all." Bob and his brother, Tuddie, were expected to go to their mother's house every weekend to clean her apartment until her death. While the Carranos welcomed the Bonifaces into their family, Rose, with her outspoken, flashy and boisterous nature never quite fit in with the much more mellow Carranos. While his brother and sister were a vital part of his life, Bob found in the Carranos a closely-knit family that he had always wished to be a part of.

Sometime in 1953, Bob's brother, Tuddie, came home from serving in the Korean War in the U.S. Army, serving under General Douglas MacArthur. Tuddie was anxious to meet his new sister-in-law and his new niece. So much had happened in Bob's life while he was away from home. In order for them to get to know one another better, Tuddie asked Nettie to join him in going to the movies to see the film *From Here to Eternity* shortly after it hit the movie theaters in August of 1953. Following their evening together, Tuddie and Nettie were equally charmed by one another. He found in Nettie a sister and a woman whom he respected and admired greatly. In Tuddie, Nettie found a brother she adored. The Carrano family equally adored Tuddie and welcomed him into the family as an honorary Carrano.

"Other than her devotion to the Carrano family, my mother was very devoted to my Uncle Tuddie, who had recently come home from the Korean War and had married Marcia Hall," Ann Marie said. "He was there for every special event and came by for dinner a lot. We would also get together with my father's sister, my Aunt Julia in Rosedale who also had children, so we would get to play with my cousins Neil and Lisa while we visited.

"The first major event I can remember was my parents brought me to Saint Catherine's Hospital for tonsil removal. My mother had on a turquoise blue coat and she was pregnant at the time. When I came home, Uncle Tuddie and my father picked me up. The day after I came home, I started throwing up blood and my parents rushed me back to the emergency room. Mom held me in the emergency room and the doctor was so inebriated that he was staggering and my mother started to scream, 'He's not going to touch my baby!' Then someone else took care of me."

On September 14, 1953, Bob left the New York City Transit Authority and became a New York City Fireman. "When my father became a fireman, he worked very long hours, but we were never lonely because the extended family was always around us," Ann Marie said. Bob was stationed in Greenpoint at the India Street firehouse, Engine Company 215, where he spent the first years of his career. Later on, he transferred to the 11th division-Brooklyn borough command- Engine Co. 229 Ladder Co. 146 located on Richardson Street. It was as "Bob the Fireman" how he came to be known and would make his career for the next twenty years. Walking under the Brooklyn-Queens Expressway, across Meeker Avenue, Bob went to work each day, loving his job and the community he served. Whether it was a prominent member of the community or a defenseless animal, Bob saved them all. No life was insignificant in his eyes. He made the cover of the newspaper saving a dog overcome by smoke in a five-alarm fire, later required emergency treatment when smoke and heat felled him during the blaze. He received citations from many animal groups for this particular heroic rescue back in 1959. Other heroic acts of Bob's include saving a torah from a burning synagogue, a priest from a burning church, a family working in their burning factory, and a family sleeping in their burning home. For that rescue, he wasn't even on duty.

Bob rescuing a dog during a blaze in Greenpoint in 1959

Although Bob's job was to save lives, he wasn't always appreciated for his acts of bravery. On time, as he was putting out a fire, he was stoned by people in the street because they wanted the building to burn so they could collect the insurance money. They caused him to receive deep gashes in his back, the stones cutting right through his fire gear. When his daughter asked him why he didn't leave the scene, he told her that no matter what, the fire had to be put out and there were lives to be saved. Mishaps did happen, as the Bonifaces had to brace themselves for in such a dangerous job. "We were all at Aunt Connie's the night before Thanksgiving one year preparing for the next day's meal when we got a call from my father from a hospital that a wall of glass had fallen on him and he was getting X-Rayed," Ann Marie said.

Bob received letters and citations for his brave acts, yet the one letter he treasured most was from a woman named Mrs. Wrieden, an eighty five -year-old woman whose father was a fireman in the latter part of the nineteenth century, who wanted to write to him to commend him for his bravery. She said, "I am so glad to know we still have such brave men like my father … God bless you and keep you well and keep doing good deeds in saving folks from fires." He kept this promise for his entire career. "My mother and us children were extremely proud of my father's work as a fireman," Ann Marie said. "He was a god in our eyes, so brave and so honorable.

"The fire department was a major part of my parents' lives. My father made many life-long friends at Engine Company 215 on India Street in Greenpoint. Mom and Dad socialized by visiting and going to barbecues with John McDonald, Walter Krzepek, who was a fire department buff, Jimmy Yaccarino, John Tirolo, Joe Ferrara, and Tom Cantirino. Much of their social life was filled with parties and barbecues with these people. Their social calendar was always filled and Mom loved it just as much as Dad did. Then Dad was transferred to Engine Company 229 Ladder Company 146 on Richardson Street where he was the chief's aide to Chief Bill Reilly. There he also made lifelong friends Mike Falabella and Harvey Hebert. We were close with them also. In fact, we used to have an annual family barbecue with the Falabellas, although Mike visited us often throughout the year because we lived so close to the firehouse."

Besides beginning a new career, Bob and Nettie also had a new place to call home. Now that Nettie was no longer working, and Maria's health was rapidly deteriorating, they decided to take an apartment that had become vacant at 147 Kingsland Avenue, just next door to Cono and Maria. In addition to taking care of her little girl and teenage son, Nettie spent a great deal of her time taking care of her mother who had helped her shoulder so many of her own heartaches over her lifetime.

Nettie looks on as her mother, Maria, sits on the front stoop of 145 Kingsland Avenue holding Ann Marie

"The word to describe my mother would be 'non-stop," Ann Marie said. "She was non-stop cleaning, cooking, and trying to take care of people. She was non-stop in taking care of her children and she took very little time to relax for herself. She would help with taking care of my grandmother Carrano every day. Aunt Rosie was still working at the time, so we would spend the day in Grandma's house. My grandmother's house was non-stop company every day of the week. Mom was very devoted to her family, as well as her birth family. She was dedicated to taking care of her mom at the end of her mother's life. This is why she took the apartment next door and ultimately the apartment above Grandma's in March of 1957."

On October 6, 1955, Nettie gave birth to her third child at the age of forty one. Susan Nancy Boniface was born at 12:05 P.M. at Brooklyn Jewish Medical Center. Susan was baptized on October 23, 1955, at Saint Cecilia's. Her godparents were Bob's brother, Tuddie, and Nettie's sister-in-law, Rose. Due to the fact that Susan was Nettie's last child, her baby, she treated her as her shining star. "My mother often referred to me as "my baby" since I was the youngest," Susan said. "When I was an adolescent that bothered me, but as I grew older I knew it was a term of endearment."

Nettie holds Susan (left) as Ann Marie looks on in 1956

In 1957, the Carranos started leaving Greenpoint. Connie and Tony and Frank and Millie both bought homes in Maspeth, Queens. Jimmy and Sally were already living in Bellport, Long Island, and Mikey and Antoinette were living between Jamaica, Queens and Florida. With Frank and Millie moving to Maspeth, the top floor apartment of 145 Kingsland Avenue was vacated. Nettie and Bob and the children moved from next door into the apartment. At this point, Maria was bed-ridden from her heart-condition. On March 10, 1957, Anthony was leaving for the Air Force. A big bon voyage party was held down the basement. All of the Carranos and Lanzettas that had helped raise him after his father's untimely death came to wish him well. Ironically, the key person in his growing up, his grandmother, Maria, was not there. She was unable to make the stairs down to the basement and remained in bed as the party was celebrated on the floor below her.

Nettie prepares to say goodbye to Anthony as he leaves for the United States Air Force on March 10, 1957

Anthony went upstairs to spend time with Maria during the party. Anthony, Nettie, Rosie, Connie, and family friend Millie Cavallo all sat in a semi-circle around Maria, propped up with pillows as she bade farewell to the grandson she had raised. Frail Maria sat on the couch with a blanket draped over her lap encircled by people who loved her. She told her grandson goodbye not for a little while, but forever. She told him that he would never see her again in this life.

Maria's health rapidly declined with every day. On May 1, 1957, Maria told Nettie that she was going to die in a week. Nettie could not accept the fact that her mother was dying. On May seventh, the doctor told Nettie that there was nothing more he could do for her mother and that it was only a matter of time. Nettie sent for a priest from Our Lady of Mount Carmel to administer last rites to her mother in Italian. That night, each of Maria's ten surviving children and their spouses came together to see her, but she was unconscious at the time.

Maria died on May 8, 1957, at 2:15 P.M. in her bed at 145 Kingland Avenue. Nettie, with her sisters Rosie, Anna, and Connie, cousin Jennie DeLuccio, and family friends Angelina Cotignola and Elvira Solomita Philip, among many others were with Maria when she died. Nettie was grief-stricken, so Jennie was her pillar of strength that day, leading her and her sisters away screaming from their mother's bedside so she could die in peace.

Father Jerome Murphy came from Saint Cecilia's to pray with them after Maria drew her last breath. Nettie's daughter, Ann Marie, was five at the time and remembers her father, Bob, taking her into Maria's bedroom where she lay dead. She knelt down with everyone else and prayed for Maria's soul. She was then sent two doors away to Mary Martino's house, but was horrified by the sight as she sat on the stoop and saw the black body bag containing her beloved grandmother being carried out the front door of her home. After the matriarch left Kingsland Avenue for the final time, "on our door was a big white crepe with a card that told you who died and the funeral arrangements," Ann Marie remembered. "It was such as sad weekend for my mother because it was Mother's Day Weekend."

"The sisters [Nettie, Rosie, Anna, and Connie] deeply loved their mother and had 'canonized' her long before she died," said Nettie's nephew, James Abramo. "They were very dedicated to their mother and deeply felt the loss upon her passing. I think it's safe to say that the brothers took it like men; little or no hysterics there. They all grieved and mourned for their mother for about a year or so and then life went on. Grandpa [Carrano] did change significantly after Grandma's death. He stopped drinking and getting drunk after her death."

Anthony was flown home from his Air Force base in Texas for Maria's wake, which was held at Greenpoint Chapel on Kingsland Avenue. Her wake was held throughout the weekend, including for Mother's Day. She was buried on May thirteenth in Saint John's Cemetery in Queens with her daughter, Carmela, whom she lost thirty-five years before. Now the grave would no longer be unmarked, as Cono and Rosie had a tombstone erected on the grave with both of their names on it.

With Maria's death, the torch was passed down to Nettie and she became the new matriarch of Kingsland Avenue. Nettie cooked for everyone in the house, including her father, Cono, Rosie, and Patty. On Fridays her brothers would visit, and like her mother, Nettie made a big pot of pasta e fagoli for them.

In the fall of 1957, Ann Marie began school at St. Cecilia's. Although she was only five year old, Nettie had went to the rectory to plead with Monsignor Reagan to take Ann Marie to school early because Bob was a fireman and needed to sleep in the day. She then added how her Uncle Robbie had been the owner of the candy store that had been next to St. Cecilia's which was now owned by St. Cecilia's to extend their property. From Nettie's urging, Monsignor Reagan relented and Ann Marie entered the first grade classroom of Sister Mary Donald in September.

Growing up on Kingsland Avenue for Nettie's children was never dull and always full of action. "We had a very busy house," Ann Marie said. "There were a lot of children on the block and we would play in front of the house. I would play with Annette, Joanne, and Angela every day. Living at 145 Kingsland Avenue was like living at the center of the universe. It was exciting to live there because there was always something going on, both before and after Grandma Carrano's death. I never regret one day living there or my parents' decision to move there. We all made our life long friends from living there."

CHAPTER SIX

MOTHERHOOD
1960 – 1969

As Mrs. Boniface, Nettie was a loyal, hard-working and devoted wife and mother. Nettie was very involved in her children's education, and both she and Bob joined the children on class trips with Saint Cecilia's and volunteering to help out the nuns. Saint Cecilia's was a very different place in the late 1950s and 1960s from when Nettie had attended there in 1920. Saint Cecilia's became a central place in Nettie's life, where she both gave of herself physically and monetarily. The Romanesque style structure was her spiritual refuge, and she could be found each weekday morning from the late 1960s on in the front left pew facing the altar, kneeling on the kneeler in prayer with her crystal rosary beads dangling from her fingers, quietly murmuring her Our Fathers and Hail Mary's. Nettie thought that Saint Cecilia's was the most beautiful church in Brooklyn and proudly told everyone it was built as a replica of Saint Cecilia's Church in Rome, where the incorrupt body of the saint is entombed. As she would leave through the side exit facing Herbert Street with her Kingsland Avenue friends, she would pause each morning in front of the statue of Saint Anthony, drop in a dime into the plastic candle, which would begin to flicker when you dropped your change in, and say a prayer to her special patron saint.

In Bob, Nettie found the love of her life. She said she had never known what love really was until the day he walked into her life. Having married a man outside of the seven blocks surrounding her own, she married someone in many ways a stark opposite to herself. Bob was gregarious with his booming voice and very charismatic. As one of Nettie's nieces remembered, Bob brought "fresh air" into the family, with his affectionate nature and constant stream of compliments. The Carrano men had always been characteristically cold and standoffish in the ways of affection. This probably can be attributed to Cono's distant relationship with all of his children. Also unlike her previous husband, Bob was a conscientious provider, never out of work and always with a steady, civil service job. She never wanted for anything. Although she remained thrifty and was always on the prowl for the best buy, Nettie kept this trait out of habit, not necessarily out of necessity.

Nettie and Bob relaxing in their living room in 1969

Her "knight in shining armor," who towered over her small stature, unlike her previous husband, was her rock and her prince. He held her on a pedestal; she was his pride and always held his awe. He was not only the love of her life, but her companion in all things. "I don't remember Mom and Dad fighting while I was growing up," Susan said. "To me they were a loving couple." With Bob, Nettie never had to face anything alone. He was at her side with full support through all of the situations that arose in the Carrano family. "I was happy when she got married again after so many years because she deserved to finally have some happiness in her life," said her sister-in-law, Rose Carrano. "She finally found happiness."

The Bonifaces on Fire Island beach.

In the years that followed Maria's death in 1957, Nettie seemed to devote part of her life to keeping Maria's memory alive and carry on her legacy, one of love, prayer, and family. She also tried to emulate many of the special qualities of her relationship with her daughters after the special moments she shared with Maria in her own youth. "One of the favorites things I liked to do when I was small was to sleep with Mommy when Daddy worked nights and when my feet were cold she had me put my feet between her legs," Susan said. "Mom said her mother used to do that for her. Many things she modeled after her mother, like eating rice with milk. She said Grandma loved that.

"At night if Ann or I would wake up and had to go to the bathroom, we'd shake Mommy and ask her to come with us. We didn't wake each other up but went right to Mommy. She never said no. Daddy always said, 'please wake me up since you know I get up for strangers,' but we never did."

On the Singer sewing machine table that stood between the two large windows of Nettie's dining room, a 5X7 colorized portrait of Maria sat of her smiling, sitting in a chair, mounted on a piece of light colored wood. From Nettie's kitchen wafted many of the smells of the recipes that had come from the kitchen below during the years when Maria carried out many meals that her progeny would remember for decades to come. Maria's large pots would sit on top of Nettie's stove as she continued her traditions of pasta e fagoli and escarole. For Christmas, Maria's large wooden board would be placed on the basement table, doused with flour, and she would begin rolling and twisting Zeppoles from the recipe her mother had carried in her head for all those years. Nettie recorded many of her recipes in a beige covered spiral notebook, which eventually passed down to Ann Marie. Every year, she rolled and twisted her Zeppoles and dropped them into the large vat of boiling oil, with the brown paper bag waiting to hold them on the counter after they were just right. She would make the dough very early in the morning, cover the top with a dishtowel and set it out to rise in the hallway. Intermittently, as the morning past, she would carefully peek to see if the yeast had been good, and how much the dough had risen. Many times on the same day, she would make her struffoli, or honey balls, as they are known. Those are balls of dough, the size of marbles that are deep fried, then saturated with honey and covered with multi-colored confections. Until the early to mid 1970s, alongside Nettie twisting the strips of dough into Zeppoles were here three sisters who had been at her side throughout the decades encompassing all of her agonies and ecstasies, Rosie, Anna, and Connie, and their sister-in-law, Rose, Rocky's wife.

Nettie and Bob with Nettie's sisters, Anna (left), Rosie (right), and Connie (second in from left) in 1950

"Aunt Nettie was one of 'the four Carrano sisters,' said nephew James Abramo. "Never have I seen four sisters that cared for each other so much, or defended each other so much, or loved each other so much. It was them against Grandpa and them against the world. Whatever hurt feelings or petty jealousies or ill will that passed between them on occasion was nothing, compared to the deep sisterly love that was there. They loved their brothers too, but there was something special about the love between those four."

"One thing Mommy always said to me, 'Never make any man come between you and your sister,' Susan said. "From this statement it is apparent of the love she had for her own sisters. They were right no matter what they did, even if we thought they were wrong. Talk about allegiance."

Then for Easter, Nettie would make her mother's recipe for pizza giene, or meat pies, as they are known. Since in Maria's day, she did not have the necessary pie pans to bake her pies, hers looked like very large calzones. Stuffed generously with dry Italian fennel sausage and smoked pork, held together by dozens of eggs. The thin crisscross strips of dough on the top of the pies made them resemble wagon wheels, and at times, they were nearly as large as them. After Nettie painted the dough with raw eggs with her little brush, they glowed a golden hue after she took them out of the oven later in the day.

The other pies she made for Easter she called "pizza gran," the sweet pie of wheat grain and clotted cheese, and a bright yellow glazed crust. The first sensation a bite into this pie gave was a sweet, citric taste, as citrus and shaved orange peels were in her recipe.

Holidays were held down the basement of Kingsland Avenue, where it was second nature to serve dinner for thirty five on a normal holiday. Cooking began days in advance. Connie, Anna, Rosie, and Rocky's wife, Rose, would usually join Nettie in preparing the feast for the massive crowd. On Thanksgiving, not only turkeys fed the masses, but trays of baked ziti, gallons of blood red wine making everyone tipsy and bursting out into song. Jimmy Carrano would play the accordion and Rosie would lead the gang in song, with favorites such as the World War I ballad that was a family favorite, *Till We Meet Again*, or "Smile the While," as they referred to it. *Let Me Call You Sweetheart* was usually not too far behind. The table would stretch the length of the basement and people either sat at the massive table or in chairs and couches that lined the walls. Kids were always running around, playing games. The trays of food on the table were endless. Beginning with nuts and fruit and ending with cakes, pastries, and coffee. The celebrations lasted for hours on end. Although not all of the Carranos were there, most attended, and the crowds grew as nieces and nephews got married or a friend or two were invited. Nettie believed that no one should ever be alone for a holiday. It was a commandment she passed down to her family.

"Holidays were busy for Mom since most of them were at our house," Susan said. "I don't remember her being nervous or upset no matter what the crowd was. One time I remember tables down the basement. It had to be a good thirty people. But she was so calm… not like me at all. Then after the meal the four sisters would be at the sink to wash, dry and put away the dishes. Deep in her heart she loved being surrounded by her family. She loved tradition and made the Zeppoles and meat pies because her mother always did. She said it didn't feel right if she didn't."

Saturdays were always an extra busy day in Nettie's house, since she had her daughters home from school to help her. "She loved a clean house and we had our chores to do on Saturday mornings," Susan said. "I remember washing the stairs and bathroom. I don't remember which end of the house I dusted. Ann did the other half. To this day when I smell the moth balls fragrance crystals I think of Mommy vacuuming." On Saturday nights she would always have a menu of roast beef, with *Rice a Roni*, and creamy mashed potatoes that could be drowned in dark brown gravy. When dinner was ready to be served, she would always summon her family to the table by saying "Okay gang." Nettie barely sat down for a bite of her sensational meal for herself. It seemed that as quickly as she served, she was clearing the table for Ann Marie to wash the dishes and Susan to dry them. "Daddy would hover over his meal so Mommy wouldn't take it away to wash the dish," Susan recalled. Then after the dishes, glasses, utensils, and pots were all washed and put away, it was bath time for Nettie's daughters. "I remember baths on Saturdays and Mom drying our hair by the stove since it was warm with the cooking of the roast beef," Susan said.

While Nettie was devoted to her family and to the Carranos, she was always busy and never had time to spend quiet time with either. “Mommy was always so busy,” Susan said. “She never sat around idle. Because she was so busy I don’t remember Mommy sitting with me to play. I remember going down Aunt Rosie’s to play. She gave me her undivided attention and played games or cards.”

“Mom was not very demonstrative,” Ann Marie said. “She would show you she loved you by doing things for you. She believed that actions spoke louder than words.”

“Mommy was a serious person,” Susan said. “What I mean is that if someone tried to play a joke on someone else, she’d never go along with it. I never knew why.” One thing that Nettie made sure she made time for with her little girls was to teach both of them their prayers. “I remember Mommy teaching me to say my prayers. We’d end our prayers with dream about the angels and all that jazz,” Susan said.

Nettie’s work at Kingsland Avenue did not take place just inside the confines of the walls of the house, but like her father, her love of the outdoors and garden led her to the small patches of dirt that she cultivated in the years after Cono’s death. “Mommy loved yard work and during the nice weather, many late afternoons were spent in her garden,” Susan said. “When it snowed we even had to make sure we had a path cleared all the way from the basement stairs to the backyard fence. Snow was an obsession with her. She wanted all snow cleared off the property, not just a path. I joined her many times in clearing it.”

Nettie and Bob were joined in their conviction of making sure their daughters had everything and that every event was special.

On the children's birthdays, Nettie came to their classrooms to bring treats for the girls to share with their classes. She and Bob also joined Ann Marie's first grade class on a trip to the Bronx Zoo, which Bob recorded on home video. Nettie and Bob would also put up their Christmas tree in the corner of the dining room, by the heavily draped windows, after the two girls had gone to bed every Christmas Eve, and then line underneath with the wall to wall presents that they had gotten. From dolls and accessories, to bicycles, clothes, tea sets, stuffed animals and board games. In the morning, bright and early, Nettie would be on the floor with the children under the tree, helping them to unwrap the gifts, or opening cardboard boxes with her large, black handled scissors, as Bob recorded the events on his eight millimeter movie camera for posterity.

When her mother-in-law, Rose Boniface and her second husband, Steve, arrived for a holiday, Nettie would accomplish all of the makings for an amazing holiday, and emerge from her bedroom looking very chic, in a beautiful dress, hair perfectly coiffed, and bejeweled. She would not be upstaged by her highly fashionable mother-in-law. "[Nettie] was a very attractive woman and her hair always was just perfect," said sister-in-law Rose Carrano, "It was always beautifully fixed. Every time I put a roller in my hair I think of her. I think she took a lot of time with her hair, how it was perfectly fixed all the time."

Nettie (shown here in 1961) made sure she always looked chic, not to be upstaged by her mother-in-law

"The most striking thing about Mommy was that she was very particular about her hair," Susan said. "She set it almost every night. When I was small she used to set my hair, too."

While Rose Boniface may have been a demanding mother and a difficult mother-in-law, she was a very devoted and generous grandmother, affectionately known by her grandchildren as "Nana," who showered all of her grandchildren with both gifts and kisses.

Each holiday began with Nettie's sister, Rosie saying grace and dousing the table and those who sat at it in holy water, as she thanked God for what they were about to receive and for the those no longer with them, and inviting those who passed before them to come joined them at the table.

Another big change that Bob brought into Nettie's life was every summer he brought her and the children away on vacations and also took many day trips to visit relatives and friends. By time Nettie had her daughters, the days of Elmont had come to an end. Anna and her husband, Charlie, had bought the property from Cono, but soon after decided to sell it. Bob took Nettie and the family different places each summer, such as the Abramo's summer home in Lake Ronkonkoma, Nettie's niece Marie's home in Hicksville, and later in Smithtown, and Nick Lanzetta's home in Bellport. "We visited Uncle Nick Lanzetta a lot in Bellport," Ann Marie said. "He had a lot of kids, so we always had a good time. My father got along well with my mother's former in-laws and everyone had a good time. We would also visit my mother's brother, Jimmy Carrano, who lived a few blocks from there."

For the summer of 1960, Bob and Nettie, along with Connie and Tony, rented a bungalow in Mastic, Long Island. The children went crabbing every day, fished for snappers, and they ate both of them nearly every night. During that summer, Nettie and Bob had many guests, including a lot of the Carranos, and even many of Bob's fireman friends. "We always went on vacations in the summer and the earliest I remember was our summer spent in Shirley," Susan said. "I slept with Mom all the time except for the nights when Daddy was off and came out to join us. One night he came out and I was being my stubborn self and screamed that I wanted to sleep with her. Daddy was livid, but Mommy calmed me down and I wound up sleeping with my cousin Francine that night. I felt so secure when I slept with Mom. It's funny but I think I slept with her the nights Dad was working right up to 1972. So I was sixteen and still sleeping with Mom.

"I remember Villa Roma where Mom watched me like a hawk at the pool. Then there's Ausable Chasm, Whiteface Mountain, Amish, Hershey, Niagara Falls. Niagara Falls was some trip. She must have been in her glory since Aunt Connie and Uncle Rocky were part of the trip. Gettysburg, too, where my cousin Bobby joined us. In Atlantic City we were joined by our family friends Laura and Nick Chiaino. It's plain to see she loved being surrounded by family and friends. Whenever we went away to a resort, I always remember her putting on her bathing suit and joining me in the pool. I felt like a million bucks that my mom was there. She didn't go in the deep water and I always made fun of her for that. But she did always try to teach me how to float, which I still can't do to this day. I remember her rubber bathing cap. She didn't like getting her hair wet."

In addition to their many vacations, Nettie and Bob and the kids enjoyed spending a great deal of time visiting their friends. "We were very close to Dad's friends Fred and Isabelle Gallo," Ann Marie said. "Mom adored them and she became just as close to them as Dad was. They were very dear and devoted friends for life. They lived in Sunset Park, Brooklyn and we often went back and forth to visit each other's homes. Fred used to bring bialys and all kinds of baked goods we couldn't get in our neighborhood.

"In 1965, the Gallos moved to Lynn, Massachusetts and Mom, Dad, Susan, and I moved with them to help them set up their new house. We stayed at least a week. It was very emotional. We were in a parking lot and how Mom and Belle cried! But for many years we visited them every year. We would have big blow-outs and all of Fred's relatives would come over.

"Mom also became close friends with Laura Chiaino, who lived two doors down from us because Susan and Laura's son, Alfred, used to play together. Mom and Laura would sit and chat every day. Then when I was going to make my First Holy Communion in 1959, Laura was a beautician and she gave me my first permanent for the occasion. The friendship between the two grew so strong, that Laura and her husband, Nick, became my parents' closest and devoted friends."

"Nettie was like a mother to me," Laura said. "Family doesn't get along as well as she and I did. I moved to Kingsland Avenue when my son, Alfred, was nine months old [in September of 1955] and we became friends through our children, Alfred and

Susan, playing together. The relationship Nettie and I had with one another was always a helpful, concerned one. When we lived next door, she would cook and send food over. Then we would sit out on the stoop and talk at night. Our husbands worked at night, so we would spend the nights together talking and keeping each other company. The friendship began as just us, and then it included our husbands and our children. We were always there for one another. She helped me a lot. We had all the holidays together. We laughed together; we cried together, we confided in one another. Although there were fifteen years between us in age, it didn't matter. There was nothing we couldn't do together. She helped me a lot. She did for me as a mother would do. She sat and listened to my problems, and I to hers, and we would help each other solve them together. We sat many a night doing that. We understood one another."

"Laura and Nick left Kingsland Avenue and moved to Uniondale, Long Island, which was another bittersweet experience for Mom, but we would all get to visit the Chiainos and they would visit us extremely often," Ann Marie said.

"Even moving away couldn't keep us apart," Laura said.

"The Chiainos became part of all of our family celebrations, many holidays, and vacations as well," Ann Marie said. "In the 1960s our families went away together, but in the 1970s, my parents went away with Laura and Nick as couples, along with my mother's brother and his wife, Uncle Rocky and Aunt Rosie Carrano."

"On one particular vacation," Laura remembered, "we went to Atlantic City. We took a room at this hotel called the Holmhurst, and we go up there, and you had to see what it looked like! The sink was right in the middle of the room. Well, anyway, we go down to the dining room for dinner, and the waiter at the door said that you could not enter without a jacket, and Bob didn't have a jacket. Now Bob was a big guy. Anyhow, the waiter brought him out a waiter's jacket to wear. He put it on and *ripppp.* They gave him another to wear and *ripppp*. After Bob ripped the second one, the waiter said 'never mind, you can come in without one.' So we went in, but how we laughed!"

"Susan asked Laura to be her confirmation sponsor because of having been so close to her since she was very small," Ann Marie said. "The whole Carrano family embraced Laura and Nick and their family as their own and their children became like cousins to us. This relationship lasted strong until the end."

"Our friendship never ceased. The only thing that took us apart was death," Laura said.

Nettie and Bob with her niece, Marie, in 1980

"Another person vital in my mother's life was her niece, Marie Mehrhof," Ann Marie said. "Marie was not only a niece of my mother, but a very close friend as well. Her children and my mother's children were around the same age. From the day Marie married her husband Ted in 1949, her home was always a place that my parents went to, first to Hicksville, Long Island and then to Smithtown. Every year during the Christmas season, Marie would come to visit with her family to see the tree at Rockefeller Center with us for many years. No matter how far away Marie lived, even when she moved to Springfield, Pennsylvania later on, the visits between my mother and her and their families was always constant. Ted and my father became great buddies as well. Marie's home in Pennsylvania became my parents' home away from home. Marie's house was always open to everybody. Although my mother loved all of her nieces dearly, she had a special bond with Marie like no other. Marie was her first niece. My mother became her aunt at eleven years old and they lived through many obstacles through life together. Their bond formed back in 1926 lasted until death."

Living at the Carrano homestead meant that the lives of Nettie and Bob were at the center of the Carrano universe. There was not a day that passed where there weren't visitors from the time they woke up in the morning until they went to sleep at night. As Anthony once said, problems were solved at 145 Kingsland Avenue, and some were caused there also. Nettie's life was an open book, as the everyday activities of her and her family took place as the rest of her family were there to witness.

By the 1960s, Nettie and Bob were holding Kingsland Avenue together single handedly. Cono, in his late eighties by this point, was starting to slow down. He entered Greenpoint Hospital on March 3, 1964, because he had lost all of the circulation in his legs. Doctors thought it would be best to amputate his legs, but Nettie and her sisters were against the idea, given the fact that their father was approaching ninety in April. Cono was a very uncooperative patient in the hospital and constantly pulled tubes out of his body. When a priest told him to pray to Jesus, he said he would only pray to Saint Cono, the patron saint of his hometown of Teggiano. During his last few days on earth, Cono told his son Patty, who worked at Greenpoint Hospital, that he was seeing members of his family who were deceased. It was clear that the end was fast approaching.

On March 19, 1964, Cono told Patty that Maria and his parents, Francesco and Rosa, had visited him that morning. Cono died that night at 8:10 P.M., a month before his ninetieth birthday. Cono had mellowed since Maria's death and had no longer caused problems with his drinking binges, which had been Maria's greatest cross for the nearly sixty years that they were married. The deaths of the Carrano patriarch, and his brother, Mike, two years later, marked the passing of the last remnants of the Old World influence on the Carrano family that Mama Rosa had brought with her across the Atlantic in 1896. Nettie and her family, her sisters and brothers, and her cousin, Jennie DeLuccio, and Jennie's daughter, Rose

Mary, were at Kingsland at the time of Cono's death. Cono's wake took place at Greenpoint Chapel and his funeral mass was at Saint Cecilia's on March twenty third at ten A.M., followed by interment at Saint John's, where he was buried with Maria and Carmela. Cono left behind ten children, thirteen grandchildren, and three great-grandchildren. Much like his Mama Rosa, Cono left behind a sour impression on his grandchildren to pass down to future generations. "Cono was respected, but not loved," Ann Marie said. "His death left no impact on his grandchildren."

"I knew Grandpa better than Grandma," James Abramo said. "I was able to speak to him a little bit on occasion and I was a teenager when he died. Grandpa continued on until 1964 getting older and, I think, a bit senile. I do recall one evening when he accidentally set a mattress on fire and Uncle Bob had to put the fire out and throw away the mattress. Aunt Nettie, Aunt Rosie and all of them were very upset. When [Rocky's son] Bobby was in the army, he visited Kingsland Avenue in uniform one day and I remember Grandpa saying in broken English "oh boy" and "be a good soldier." When he was hospitalized in 1964, the doctors inserted a Foley Catheter into him. He didn't understand what this was about and he ended up pulling it out. This caused much damage to his bladder and penis. I think he eventually died during that hospitalization.

"I think they all mourned the loss of their father but probably no one was really sorry to see him gone. He had been a drunk and a tough and difficult man to live with for many years and had probably abused Grandma in different ways through those many years. They never 'canonized' their father, that's for sure. Shortly after his death, many changes happened at Kingsland Avenue. The place was cleaned up and modernized. The old dump in the back yard was disposed of and the yard was modernized. I don't think they mourned his loss as much as they mourned hers. In fact, to a certain degree, some were probably thankful that he was gone."

The children of Maria and Cono were also growing old. On January 7, 1966, Patty suffered a stroke at home in his sleep. He was left mute and paralyzed on his left side. Confined to a wheelchair for the rest of his life, Patty went to live in a nursing home, eventually settling in Van Doren Nursing Home in Queens, after having been at a few others. His lived for fifteen years in this shell of his former self and died at the age of eighty on August 9, 1981. "Dad and Mom had helped Aunt Rosie a great deal in settling Uncle Pat in the nursing home and keeping track of his paperwork and making all the necessary phone calls," Ann Marie said. Patty's stroke marked the beginning of the nursing home era and the beginning of the deterioration of the Carrano family.

Another cross that came to weigh heavily on Nettie and Bob's shoulders had been a bone of contention since before her first marriage. The ongoing battle between Jimmy and Sally Carrano had reached epic proportions. While Sally traveled the world, Jimmy drank, took drugs, went crazy, and shot both a picture of Sally and also shot himself! "Jimmy got addicted to drugs and he had them everywhere," said brother-in-law Nick Lanzetta. "He threatened to come over and kill ya. Their problems started early in their marriage. He was very jealous and suspicious."

"One time he took iodine, shot his picture," sister-in-law Betty Lanzetta said. "He called me and said 'Betty, I think I shot myself. The bullet was still inside of him. He had a good heart, he was a good person."

With Jimmy out of control, he came home to live at Kingsland Avenue. Nettie and Bob took care of getting him settled and back on track, even setting him up with an apartment nearby. Then Sally made a trip to Brooklyn to woo her husband back. After that, Nettie and Bob washed their hands of the situation. Jimmy and Sally moved to Greenbelt, Maryland close by to their children, Sally Ann and Mary Lou and their families. After a visit in the mid-1970s and Sally's visit to stay at Kingsland Avenue with Nettie for James Abramo's wedding to his wife Linda in 1978, Nettie never saw Jimmy and Sally again. Jimmy went into a nursing home due to dementia and died there on January 7, 1985 at the age of seventy seven. On his last Thanksgiving, Sally Ann called Nettie so Jimmy could speak to her. She and Rosie spoke to him on the two extensions and Nettie's voice cracked with emotion as she spoke to her brother after a very long time. When he died two months later, he was cremated and Sally Ann brought his ashes home to Kingsland Avenue. Nettie, Rosie, Anna, and Connie each spent time with the box wrapped with silver paper and adorned with flowers. Together on a wintry Saturday morning at the end of January, with overcast skies and a snow covered ground, the remaining Carranos gathered in the chapel of St. John's Cemetery for Jimmy's interment in the Carrano plot, as Nettie fulfilled Jimmy's dying wish, to be with his Momma.

Nettie and her family continued to live at Kingsland Avenue. She sent her daughters, Ann Marie and Susan, to Saint Cecilia's School around the corner, where Anthony and most of her nieces and nephews had attended. "I remember the first day of school and knew I didn't want to leave my mother, as she was my refuge," Susan said, "so I screamed and carried on, only to look at her smiling face as we first graders walked out of the room. She tried to reason with me that I'd come home soon. Didn't I remember that Ann Marie comes home every day? I finally caught on and then lunch times were always prepared with hot lunches. She made the forty five minutes we were home so special. As I grew older, Ann and I would walk down Kingsland Avenue, but I'd see my mother's head hanging out the window until we reached the corner."

Ann Marie graduated Saint Cecilia's in 1965 and went onto The Mary Louis Academy, but after a year and a half transferred to Saint Nicholas High School in Williamsburg. In June 1969, Ann Marie graduated from Saint Nick's and Susan graduated the valedictorian of her class at Cecilia's, winning the Trunz Scholarship, which Nettie was enormously proud of. Nettie and Bob had a graduation party for both of them in the yard of Kingsland Avenue. Ann Marie went on to New York City Community College and Susan went on to The Mary Louis Academy in Jamaica, Queens.

Nettie with her daughters Susan (left) and Ann Marie (right) on their graduation day in 1969

Not long after the girls' graduations, Bob's mother, Rose, died from a stroke in Wyckoff Heights Hospital on July 18, 1969, at the age of sixty seven. Bob came in late that night and told his family, "We lost Momma." Rose Boniface's wake was held at Abramo Funeral Home, but on July twentieth, everyone left early and went to Kingsland Avenue to see Neil Armstrong walk on the moon. Rose was buried with her first husband and mother in her family plot in Saint John's Cemetery. As the 1960s drew to a close, both of Nettie's and Bob's parents were deceased.

CHAPTER SEVEN

MATRIARCH
1970 – 1977

As the 1970s were ushered in, Nettie not only saw the Carranos get older, but the next wave of their children get married and begin the next generation. In 1970, Connie and Tony's daughter, Francine, got married in May, followed by Rocky and Rose's son, Bobby, on November fifteenth. When Ann Marie attended the wedding, she was on her first date with one of her new friends that she made that year. His name was Peter Franzese and he was from Calyer Street.

Ann Marie had met Peter a few months before while hanging out on Frost Street at his cousin's house. Not long after they met, Ann Marie and a group of their friends were in a car crash after a night hanging out in Manhattan.

"We went out with my friends to this place called Doctor Generosity in Manhattan and when we got in the car and headed for home, two taxi cabs hit us," Ann Marie remembered. "Two of the girls were hurt pretty badly. I saw it coming and braced myself, but I got a concussion anyhow and multiple cuts.

"I exited the car and saw a phone booth. When I went to go to the phone booth to call my parents, I passed out. When I opened my eyes, I was being wheeled into Lenox Hill Hospital. When my parents were notified, my father informed them that he was a New York City fireman and for them to please tell him exactly how I was. They told him that I had a concussion, but I would be okay. Later on, my parents told me that they got dressed, got in the car, and didn't speak a word to one another until they got to the hospital. When they walked into my room, I got hysterical crying with relief when I saw them. They said I reminded them of a little girl. I was released about six thirty that morning."

The next day, Peter, along with his cousin, Jimmy, went to Kingsland Avenue to see how Ann Marie was doing. "There was an army there," Peter said. "Jimmy and I sat in the parlor. Ann Marie came out to see us and we had a conversation, then we left. The next time I went there was when she had to register for school, she was very discombobulated. Her mother and father thought it was the greatest thing that I would go with her to register for her classes. When we came back, her father said how nice it was that I would help Ann Marie like that. Then I used to walk her home and sit on the stoop, talking with her for hours. Then we started going out.

"Ann Marie's mother wasn't a real conversational person. She cooked, cleaned, and gardened. Ann Marie's father interacted and talked about things. Her mother's world revolved around the house, she just did her thing."

A year later, Ann Marie and Peter were still going out, and on the steps of Saint Cecilia's school, he asked Ann Marie to marry him. "Her father wanted to have wine and cheese with me to hear my intentions with Ann Marie," Peter said. "We talked about my future." Following their wine and cheese conversation, Ann Marie and Peter were engaged to be married at the close of 1971.

Along with the marriages came the passage of time. On the Fourth of July 1970, Nettie's "Prince Charming" from her childhood succumbed to bone cancer. Frank Carrano-the oldest of Maria and Cono's eleven children-died at his Maspeth home at the age of seventy one. Nettie was overwrought with emotion over the illness and death of her brother, whom she had both idolized and fancied to be her father during his first marriage, since her relationship with her own father was nearly non-existent. Nettie had always looked up to Frank with sheer admiration, never losing that hero-worship she felt when she was a three year old girl trying to find Frank among the sailors marching through Greenpoint so many years before.

Following Frank's death, Mike's wife, Antoinette was stricken with lung cancer, although neither she nor Mike ever smoked in their lives. As her illness ravaged her body, she went to live with her sister, Millie, who took care of her at the end of her illness in her Ridgewood home. In the meantime, Mike came home to live at 145 Kingsland Avenue in Rosie's apartment, while spending each day at Antoinette's bedside. Mike would ask Ann Marie's boyfriend, Peter, to drive him to his sister-in-law's house to be with his dying wife. Then in the meantime, he said Peter could use the 1966 Chevy Nova as he wished.

Antoinette died on August 3, 1972 at the age of sixty five. Although she had not lived in Greenpoint for decades, her wake was held on Kingsland Avenue at the Greenpoint Chapel. Mike made Kingsland Avenue his permanent residence following Antoinette's death. He became an active member of Nettie's family and much loved especially by Ann Marie and her fiancé, Peter. Since their wedding was planned for the upcoming May, Mike had promised the couple his green 1966 Chevy Nova as a wedding present. While he was happy living in Greenpoint behind the walls of the Carrano family homestead, the pain of Antoinette's death completely devastated him. Unlike any of his brothers, Mike was a deeply religious man who attended mass daily, and was known to sit and pray with his mother throughout their lives together.

Mike underwent coronary bypass surgery at the beginning of 1973. He survived the surgery, but slipped into a coma, dying on January 19, 1973 at the age of sixty nine. While he would be conspicuously missed at Ann Marie and Peter's upcoming wedding, his generous gift would be a fond reminder of him always. They kept his car until 1988.

While it was painful for Nettie to begin burying her siblings one by one, she was not ready for tragedy to strike her own family. Bob had been diagnosed with diabetes in 1969, at the age of forty two. On February 7, 1972, after dropping Susan off at school, Bob walked into the apartment an ashen color and feeling quite ill. "Dad looked steel gray and he called his fireman friend, Harvey, and said he thought he was having a heart attack," Ann Marie said. "Then he asked Anthony to take him to the hospital."

"Momma and I took Dad to St. John's Hospital in Queens," Anthony said. "They took him right away. Doctor LoPresti wasn't at the hospital, but said to get him there right away. They checked Dad out and sent him up immediately. He didn't really have to wait for a bed."

When Doctor LoPresti finally came to see Nettie and Anthony, he informed them that Bob had suffered an infarction, a massive heart attack that nearly claimed his life. He told them that there would be a slow recovery ahead and no guarantees for the future. Ann Marie rushed to John Jay College to tell Peter about her father and they both rushed to St. John's Hospital. When they got there, they found Nettie and Tuddie in the waiting room. "We didn't know if he would live or die," Peter said. "Everyone was very concerned; he was the head of the family. Uncle Tuddie being there was very comforting. He said to me 'my brother has a very high regard for you.' Because Dad had the heart attack, Mom took over the reigns of power of the family. When she took over, she became more involved with what was going on in the family."

"It was a Monday and Dad had brought me to school," Susan remembered. "When I got home, Uncle Tuddie was there and said 'Come here, Susan' and took me into the hallway and said 'I wanted to let you know that your father had a heart attack, but he's all right.' It was very comforting to have Uncle Tuddie there. Mom was beside herself because Dad was never sick before."

After a hospital stay that stretched into weeks, Bob finally came home from the hospital. Indeed, he had a very slow recovery ahead of him. When he was released from the hospital, he was taken off active duty on the fire department. When he did come home though, scores of cards and baskets from all his friends from the fire department awaited his return. “I never saw a person get so many cards,” Ann Marie said.

Following his heart attack, Bob was never able to work again, and became part of the every day goings on at Kingsland Avenue. “Dad never worked again and was always home,” Ann Marie said. “As time passed, he got crankier and sometimes he and Mom bickered, which they never did before. As he got better though, he became part of Mom’s every day home life and even picked up some of the chores.”

While Nettie and Bob’s life had always been on the go, ready to help others and a fairly free schedule, many of their every day outings and appointments on their calendars were now for doctor’s appointments. “Mom was devastated by this because she had always seen Dad as such a strong man, and the reality now was that he was really a very sick man,” Ann Marie said. “His heart attack was so severe that he could never work again. This was made worse because he suffered from diabetes. From then on, his days were spent largely on the couch watching television.”

Bob’s heart attack did change the way how many things were done at Kingsland Avenue. Without Bob as her rock and support to pull off many of the events she hosted for the Carranos, she had to bow out as host to the large holidays and parties she had hosted for so many years down the basement. Following Bob’s 1972 heart-attack, all of the Carranos had their holidays on their own. Even the Grand Central Station atmosphere of the constant stream of visitors in and out of the house thinned out considerably.

The Bonifaces had quieter holidays after Bob's heart attack, like they did in this picture for Thanksgiving 1976

After a second episode with his heart, Bob urged Ann Marie and Peter to move up their wedding date from September to May, just in case he didn't have much time ahead of him.

Nettie and Bob in 1973

On Saturday, May 5, 1973, flanked by her son, Anthony and her godson, Joseph Rizza, Connie's son, Nettie proudly walked down the aisle to her seat in the front pew of Saint Cecilia's. As she looked down the aisle from her pew, Nettie proudly watched her daughter, Ann Marie, walk down the aisle on Bob's arm to be given away to Peter Franzese. Memories of Nettie's two weddings down that same aisle must have filled Nettie's mind as she saw her daughter now at the altar to become Ann Marie Franzese. The 4:30 P.M. ceremony was performed by Father Matthew Diamond. The witnesses were Peter's cousin, James, whose house it was where Ann Marie and Peter met, and Ann Marie's sister, Susan. The ceremony was followed by a reception at the Polonaise Terrace on Greenpoint Avenue in Greenpoint. Peter's father, Sam, drove the newlyweds to the airport the next day for their honeymoon at Cove Haven in the Poconos.

The Boniface family at Ann Marie and Peter's wedding in 1973

Peter Franzese, born September 5, 1950, at the now closed St. John's Long Island City Hospital in Long Island City, New York, is the only child from the marriage of Pasquale (Pat) Franzese and Rose Marie Porti. Peter's mother, Rose, died three days before his first Christmas. When he was six months old, Peter went to live with his father's brother, Sam, and his wife, Josephine, when they bought their new home on Calyer Street in Greenpoint. It is there that he would be raised as their son, along with the three daughters they had after Peter came to live with them. Peter attended Saint Anthony's school in Greenpoint, the archrival school of Ann Marie's beloved Saint Cecilia's. He graduated from John Jay College of Criminal Justice the year before.

A month after Ann Marie and Peter's wedding; Susan graduated from The Mary Louis Academy. She enrolled at Baruch College that fall in Manhattan, where she studied business administration. The granddaughter of illiterate immigrants, Susan would receive her B.B.A. in the spring of 1977, the first female college graduate in the family.

When Ann Marie and Peter returned from their honeymoon, they took an apartment at 90 Monitor Street, just across Meeker Avenue from Nettie. Ann Marie woke up many mornings to find her mother had been there while they were sleeping and find rolls and bagels on the table. In fact, while she and Peter would be at work, Nettie would take their dirty laundry to her house to wash. "Mom helped us get that apartment in February of 1973 and even negotiated the rent for us," Peter said. "She would come to our apartment, let herself in with the key, take our dirty clothes, bring them home and wash and fold them, and bring them back. Ann Marie said to her once, suppose we don't have any clothes on when you come in? Her mother said to us 'nothing shocks me!' We always laughed about that."

Nettie with Susan, Ann Marie, and Peter on Thanksgiving 1973

Nineteen months after his heart attack, Bob retired on Nettie's fifty ninth birthday from the fire department. The department held a testimonial dinner in Bob's honor at the Polonaise Terrace in Greenpoint on November 9, 1973, where they not only paid tribute to his many years of dedication and devotion to the brotherhood as a New York City firefighter, but also to Nettie, who they dubbed the "meatball lady" for having shared her memorable and delicious meals with Bob's co-workers over the past twenty years.

On April 29, 1975, Nettie and Bob celebrated their silver wedding anniversary. Their children decided to throw them a surprise party down the basement, where their wedding reception was held. On the day of the party, Nettie and Bob had driven out to Uniondale to visit Laura and Nick Chiaino, who knew that there was going to be the party later in the day. “When they came by me,” Laura said, “I knew they were having the party and I didn’t like what Nettie was wearing. She wasn’t dressed how I thought she should for a party, since she didn’t know she was going to be having one. So I told her, ‘Nettie, put on this blue pants suit instead, because we’re going out.’ So she did and we went to the party.” Nettie was in shock to find out when she returned home to Kingsland Avenue that the reason she was wearing Laura’s outfit was to celebrate her anniversary with a basement full of family and friends.

Also in 1975, Ann Marie and Peter left Greenpoint and bought their own home. The two story colonial in Richmond Hill, Queens was one house off the corner of 97th Avenue on 130th Street. While Ann Marie and Peter were at work at Greenpoint Hospital, Nettie and Bob would drive over to their new home and work on different projects to make the house the showcase their daughter and her husband dreamed it to be. “They came over our house and put up Sanitas wall coverings, paneling, or even paint,” Peter remembered. “They felt like it was their house. Mom would put on an old pair of shoes and garden, pull weeds, or even paint the fence with silver paint. If you needed something from her, you got it. We started doing projects together. If she had a project, no one would really help her. She knew if she asked me for something, that I would never say no.”

Nettie with son-in-law Peter working on the backyard in Richmond Hill, Queens in 1975

A year later, Ann Marie and Peter got a beagle-terrier named Mikey. Whenever Nettie and Bob's car pulled up the carport in Richmond Hill, Mikey would start to cry. Nettie would always bring a plastic bag full of some treats for him, so as soon as she came through the door, he would put his head in her bag, looking to see what treats she had brought for him. Then he would put his mouth on her arm and tug her to wherever he wanted to bring her. One time he tugged too hard though and ripped her leather coat. When he would get mischievous, he would grab one of Rosie's slippers, when she joined Nettie and Bob during their visits, and she would run through the rooms after the dog trying to retrieve it. Although

Nettie loved Mikey, she turned to Ann Marie one day and said, "Is this what I have to look forward to for grandchildren?"

Nettie with Mikey, Ann Marie and Peter's dog

On September 12, 1976, Mary Lanzetta, Nettie's former mother-in-law that had left her penniless following her husband's tragic death nearly forty years before, died at the age of eighty nine in Patchogue, Long Island. Although she had not lived in Greenpoint for many years, Mary had arranged for her wake and funeral to take place in the neighborhood she had spent her youth. While her wake took place on Kingsland Avenue at Greenpoint Chapel, Nettie opened her home to her former in-laws, who had remained active members in her life throughout the years.

While Nettie was estranged from her sister-in-law, Sally, she remained close with her brother-in-law, Nick, and sister-in-law Rose until death. With Bob and Anthony, Nettie returned with the Lanzettas to the site of the tragedy of 1939, when on the last morning in May, two caskets were lowered and two widows mourned the sudden and tragic blast that changed their lives forever. While Mary Lanzetta had been a cruel and heartless mother-in-law to Nettie, she remained a part of Nettie's life until the time of her death. She saw Mary often, during her many visits with Bob and her children to Nick's house in Bellport every summer. Nick remained like a brother to Nettie and never forgot to call Nettie every birthday on September fifteenth. He also took Anthony every summer to stay at his house, always a dutiful godfather and uncle, taking an interest in the lives of all his nieces and nephews, until today at the age of eighty seven.

For Nettie, 145 Kingsland Avenue was more than a house. It represented her parents and the glue that had held the Carrano family together. She worked desperately to hold together the family as her mother had for so many decades. As the years were passing, everyone was beginning to go their separate ways and the siblings were dying one by one.

Nettie's Tara, 145 Kingsland Avenue

The family home front was and always would be 145 Kingsland Avenue. When Cono died in 1964, he left its soul ownership to his daughter, Rosie. By 1977, the house was run and maintained by Nettie and Bob. Rosie was getting on in years and unable to uphold the responsibilities of the house. In that year, Nettie decided she wanted to buy the house from Rosie. Given the fact that Rosie never married, her estate at her death would be spit among the living siblings. Many were concerned that they get the highest price for the house and that it would affect their inheritance. For the first time in Nettie's life, she was horrified and devastated to see the division in the family, and behind her back, was torn to pieces by those against her buying the property and the price she would pay for it. In the end, for better or worse, she paid the going rate for the house, with a clause. The clause stated that along with the ownership of the property, she would take on the full responsibility for Rosie, who would live there rent free, until the time of her death.

Susan graduated from Baruch College in June of 1977 and began looking for a job a month later. While she walked the sidewalks of New York in search of employment, she began having a nagging leg pain. "My left knee was hurting a bit, but I struck it up to a lot of walking the pavements of Manhattan," Susan said. "I went to the doctor in August and he told me to put a hot compress on it and I should feel better. But after scrubbing the floor on my hands and knees and going camping with my friend, Diane, I developed severe pain. So back to the doctor I went in late September. He sent me for x-rays and the answer came in on October fourth. I was diagnosed with a giant cell tumor of the left tibia. I landed in Wyckoff Heights Hospital on my birthday, October sixth, but had to be released and then was re-admitted to Lenox Hill Hospital on Halloween. The whole billing issue from my stay at Wyckoff was a nightmare. But thank God for my father, he managed to clear things up. Physically, I'm certain that Mom was really worried about me. I was just twenty one and what did I know about a possible bad outcome? Mom kept her worry to herself and didn't really let on to me. The whole family was on edge about my biopsy, so when the results came back benign, everyone was overjoyed. Mommy could breathe out. It had been noted on the x-rays that this was 'a rare instance.' Mommy had originally been slated to have surgery with me. When Doctor Lewis in Lenox Hill Hospital realized that my left tibia bone needed to be scraped out, he said my mother's pelvic bone would be scraped and put into my leg. At the time he didn't think my pelvis could do it. But as it turns out, my pelvis was shaved and part of my pelvic bone is now in my tibia. Mommy was more than willing to help me out with her bone if I needed, did I require it. In retrospect, I'm very glad I was able to suffice on my own because the recuperation of the both of us would not have been a pretty picture.

"Thank God all turned out well, but I had a three month recuperation in front of me. With the cast from thigh to toe and not being able to put any pressure on it for all but the last two weeks, my road ahead wasn't so much fun. I felt bad not being able to do anything, so Mommy sewed me kind of like an apron with a pocket so I could put things in it. I remember trying to set the table a few times dish by dish. I didn't want Mommy waiting on me hand and foot, although she did it as much as she could. She and Daddy came to visit me often while I was in the hospital, but I honestly don't remember how long I was there. I just remember the surgery was November fourth. I remember being very relaxed during the three month recuperation and Mommy never made me feel bad or guilty."

Also in June, Nettie and Bob were not ready to receive the devastating news that hit one of their pillars of strength through the years. Bob's brother, Tuddie, was diagnosed with lung cancer, and spent the next six months in and out of the hospital. Bob and Nettie spent a great deal of time at Tuddie's side, in addition to taking care of Susan and working on the finalization of purchasing 145 Kingsland Avenue from Rosie. Susan remembered visiting Tuddie during one of his hospital stays: "On one visit to the doctor, Dad, Mom, and I detoured to see Uncle Tuddie at New York Hospital. There I was in a wheelchair, but we had a nice visit. Mommy really felt bad about Uncle Tuddie, since she liked him so much."

On December first, Tuddie was admitted to New York Hospital once again, only now in the advanced stages of his cancer bout. While Tuddie laid clinging to life and gasping for air into his cancer filled lungs, Ann Marie received the news that she was going to have a baby. When Tuddie heard the news, he was delighted. Ann Marie had suffered a miscarriage the year before and had concerns for her new pregnancy. The day before his last on earth, Tuddie told Bob that there was nothing to fear with Ann Marie's new pregnancy, because she was going to have a healthy child, and it was going to be a boy. "When Dad came home that day and told Mommy what Uncle Tuddie has said, Mommy grinned from ear to ear," Susan said. Then on the morning of December 9, 1977, Nettie and Bob received a call to get to New York Hospital, Tuddie had taken a turn for the worse. They were at Tuddie's side when he died that morning at 10:45 A.M. on the anniversary of his mother Rose's birthday. Tuddie was forty seven years of age, leaving behind a wife and three children, and the three children he had with his first wife, Marcia. "Mom was very upset when *the* call came about Uncle Tuddie," Susan said. "She was right there for Dad."

While Nettie and Bob were weary from the loss of a treasured brother and relieved by the close call with their daughter, as 1977 drew to a close, Nettie and Bob anxiously awaited the birth of their first grandchild.

CHAPTER EIGHT

NANA
1978 – 1986

As 1978 rolled in, a blast of relentless snowfall rolled in its wake. With Susan in a full leg cast following her surgery and Bob's heart condition, Nettie, although only five feet tall, bravely trudged out into snow, shoveling so constantly, she was teased for being out there with her shovel to catch the snowflakes. Susan remembered the storms of 1978 and Nettie's work to keep 145 Kingsland Avenue from being buried in the mounds of white.

"The winter of 1978 was brutal," Susan said. "It was very icy and snowy. I had a hard time getting around and needed to be carried whenever I went out. I felt bad about not being able to help Mom shovel. Even though my cast came off on January thirtieth, when it snowed eighteen inches on February sixth, on top of the sixteen inches on January twentieth, which caused mail delivery to be cancelled for two days, Mommy did all the shoveling herself. I always felt bad about that."

Delight and relief must have filled Nettie when Susan's cast was finally removed at the beginning of 1978. While the loss of her dear brother-in-law, Tuddie, in December still cast a dark shadow on their lives, she and Bob had a lot to be grateful for in 1978. They were both very grateful that the tumor in Susan's leg had been benign, after many days and nights of worry. They were also anxiously awaiting the coming of their first grandchild, due on July twentieth. Bob and Nettie brought Ann Marie to her appointments to Doctor Drezga as her pregnancy progressed. Nettie was with Ann Marie when she heard the heart beat of the baby in Ann Marie's womb for the first time. She marveled at how pregnancy had changed in the years since she had her three children, and the miracle of hearing the heart beat of her yet unborn grandchild.

Then in the early hours of Monday, June 5, 1978, Ann Marie called Nettie to say that her due date was here, now that the contractions were getting closer together. The baby was on its way. On May twenty sixth, "Ann Marie called to say she was going to give birth earlier than July twentieth; Mommy was **so** excited," Susan said. "I remember her saying 'I'm going to be a nanny!'"

Following Ann Marie's phone call, Nettie, Bob, and Susan piled into the car and headed for Ann Marie and Peter's Richmond Hill home. "I remember it being very quiet in the car when the three of us rushed over when Ann Marie went into labor," Susan said. At six A.M., it was time to go to Booth Memorial Medical Center in Flushing, Queens for the birth. Nettie and Bob got into their car and followed Peter, in his jeep with Ann Marie, and Susan, heading to the hospital. Susan tried to do breathing exercises with Ann Marie, but Ann Marie snapped at her as the contractions got worse during the ride.

As Nettie waited with Bob and Susan in the waiting room, Ann Marie gave birth to her first child. At 9:13 A.M., Nettie became a "Nanny." Seven and a half weeks premature, Peter Michael Franzese was born, weighing only four pounds six ounces and 17 ½ inches long. Just as Tuddie had prophesized, Ann Marie gave birth to a healthy, premature son, who was born on the feast day of Saint Boniface.

"One thing we all thought was that Ann Marie was going to be dramatic, but as it turned out, she gave birth to Peter Michael like a trooper," Susan said. "Mommy was just so excited when Peter was born. She was broken hearted, as was Ann Marie, that he was so small and couldn't come home right away."

Over the next few weeks, I, Peter Michael, grew stronger every day.

I came down with yellow jaundice two days after my birth, the same day my mother, Ann Marie, was released from the hospital, and was placed in an incubator for four days. In the process I even lost my six ounces. Luckily I did not have any birth defects, but had to gain weight. My mother was devastated when she went home a few days after my birth because she had to leave her baby behind, unlike most of the other mothers. My hospital stay lasted for my first eighteen days of life. During that time, my mother made two visits every day to the hospital for all of my feedings, persisting to get me to ingest my one to two ounces of formula at each feeding. My Nana Nettie and Grandpa Bob brought her to the feedings and visited me constantly-probably my most frequent visitors after my parents-during my extended hospital stay. Then, on June twenty third, I was finally released from the hospital and came home to my Richmond Hill home for the first time. As my parents brought me through the threshold of 97-12 130th Street for the first time, not far behind them were Nana Nettie, Grandpa Bob, and Aunt Susan, ready to help and overjoyed that I was home at last.

Nettie holds Peter the day he comes home from the hospital in June 1978

"When you did come home, I remember Nana helping your mom prepare the food and bottles," Susan said to me. "I also remember Nana being actively involved in decorating the new baby's room. I can't say for sure, but she might have done some painting. I say this since she liked to paint and Grandpa Bob would make fun and say that if you stood still long enough and were in her painting path, she'd paint you too!"

On August 5, 1978, I was baptized at St. Benedict Joseph Labre Church in Richmond Hill, Queens, by my father's childhood friend, Father Gregory Weilukski. My godparents were my Aunt Susan and Joseph Rizza, Nana's sister, Connie's son. A few days later, on August fourteenth, Susan was hired by AT&T. "When I got hired at AT&T," Susan said, "I had to call Mommy every morning when I got to work. One morning, when she got out of bed, she fell out scrambling to get the phone. I told her she shouldn't do that or else I'd stop calling. But I know she was proud of me on getting my job. The phone company was really a man's job at that time but I was a female and I made it. She made sure I always brought lunch so I didn't have to eat food on the outside. She bought me fresh rolls for breakfast once I started to work so I didn't have to buy them outside and spend my money. I know she worried about me traveling the trains alone so early in the morning. And then she knew the neighborhood I was in since the previous year we had both gone to see her brother, Uncle Rocky, at Saint Clare's and remarked to each other 'boy… this is some neighborhood.' After all, it was called Hell's Kitchen. I felt kind of bad when I had to tell her where I was working. I remember coming home and saying, "Hey Mom, remember last year when we went to visit Uncle Rocky? Well, her face dropped."

As 1978 drew to a close, Nettie was overjoyed over the addition to her life. She was now a Nana, a role she waited anxiously to be hers and relished when she was given the title. She was also relieved to see Susan settled into her career, now that her leg was healed and she had gone back to a normal life. Nettie and Bob, along with Susan, had a lot to celebrate the Christmas of 1978 with their new grandson on his first Christmas.

Every morning Nettie rose before the sun, soundlessly getting out of bed, making her way through her room, Susan's room, the living room, dining room, and into the kitchen. At the flip of a switch, the fluorescent dome light above would flood the room with light. She would go to the sink, take out her washboard from the cabinet underneath the sink, and wash her clothes as frigid water ran from the tap and the sink filled with suds, as she began her daily chores. Nettie's icy hands would wring out the excess water from her garments, and then she would take them to the large kitchen window.

As the inky sky began to fill with a scarlet color from the rising sun, Nettie would see the same site she had seen for decades. Across her yard, she saw the verdigris steeple of Saint Cecilia's, pigeon cotes on the Formato's rooftop, and on the other side of the Brooklyn-Queens Expressway, the steeple of St. Stanislaus Church, and beyond that, the skyline of the city nearest and dearest to her heart of all. She would see the Empire State Building and the majestic World Trade Center, or the Twin Towers, as she always referred to them, that she had watched soar higher and higher into the sky each day, until their completion in 1973. She had also stood at this window on October 3, 1979, and looked on as Pope John Paul II rode by on the Brooklyn-Queens Expressway and blessed her little town in Brooklyn. He even visited St. Stanislaus Church in

Greenpoint during his New York visit. She had stood at the window with Ann Marie and her year old grandson, Peter. Three generations would witness the Holy Father's visit together at the window, as Bob and Peter Sr. looked on from the roof.

Nettie would lean out the window and begin clipping her clothes to the white rope clothesline that was attached to the house and a tall, skinny black ladder across the yard in the middle of her garden. The high pitched squeal from the pulley could be heard as the clothes moved across the sky above the cement yard below, fluttering and jouncing as they hung to dry in the morning Brooklyn sunshine.

Nettie in the kitchen during her morning rituals in 1983

When her clothes were hung to dry, and waiting with anxious anticipation for Susan's phone call that she had arrived safely to work in Manhattan, Nettie would take out her long handled, black pot with white specks. She would fill it with tap water and place it on the black grate of the gas jet, where the blue flame appeared after a few clicks from turning the knob. As the water-filled pot sat above the blue flame, Nettie would go into her pantry, a closet that was once a dumbwaiter, which housed all of her dishes, mugs, and plates. Out she would take a mug and a small yellow saucer and place them on the table. Already on the table sat the white plastic container that held sugar, *Sweet 'N Low*, and instant coffee. A scoop of instant coffee went in the bottom of her mug, followed by a saccharine tablet or packet of *Sweet 'N Low*, waiting for the eternity of the water to boil. Then the hissing and rolling of the water would alert her that the water had come to a boil. As smoke escaped from the pot, Nettie carefully and deftly poured the water into her waiting cup, letting it set to both brew and cool. Never fully satisfied by how much it would cool, Nettie would pour some coffee into her little yellow saucer, and sip at it a little at a time.

After her morning coffee, Bob would still be sleeping well into the morning, since he stayed up to watch the late, late, late show, and being alone in the apartment, Nettie would get ready for her day, being washed and dressed some time before seven. By 7:45 A.M., grabbing her crystal rosary from the Lazy Susan that sat under the mirror in the dining room, Nettie would start making her way to daily mass.

When she got down to the stoop, her Kingsland Avenue chums Jeannie and Annie would be in front of their houses as well. Together they would chat as they walked the length of Kingsland Avenue and turned onto Herbert Street to enter the side entrance for the eight A.M. mass at St. Cecilia's.

Dipping her fingers into the white marble font, Nettie would make the sign of the cross. After touching the foot of St. Anthony of Padua, she made her way to the front pew on the Herbert Street side of St. Cecilia's, where she sat and reflected, praying for her sick husband, her children, grandson, and the living and deceased Carranos, as she did each morning. As she sat and listened to the readings and the homily of the officiating priest, the crystal rosary beads slipped through her fingers and she silently made her prayers to Our Lady, whose statue she always sat in front of. On Mondays she would stay after mass for the Novena of Our Lady of the Miraculous Medal.

On her way home from morning mass, Nettie would often stop at George's Meat Market on Kingsland Avenue, where she would buy cold cuts and Italian bread, among other items that she could conveniently get when she didn't go to the supermarket. She would be careful about her prices, staying away from items she felt were "very dear," or exorbitantly priced.

She would carry home her bags from George's, usually brown paper bags inside white "I Love New York" plastic ones; she would walk down Kingsland Avenue towards home, stopping and chatting with neighbors that happened to be out front, either sitting outside or sweeping the front of their homes.

By time she returned home, Nettie would go into the first floor apartment to check in on her sister, Rose. By this time she would be getting up and probably waiting for a pot to boil on her stove for instant coffee as well. After a few minutes checking in down there, Nettie would go up the flight of stairs to put away her groceries and start on her chores of the day.

“Mommy was always so busy,” Susan said. “She never sat around idle. She’d do a clothes line full of wash by hand. As an adult when everyone was still alive I wondered why she wasn’t tired in the evening and wondered if I’d have that energy when I was her age.”

Bob always referred to Nettie as the woman of a thousand changes. Characteristically, she changed her outfit as many as five times a day. Once she came home from church, she would change her outfit from a pants suit to a pair of black slacks and a smock. She had a vast variety of house smocks, some more dressy with vibrant colors and puffed sleeves, or others less fancy for when she went out to work on her backyard garden. Nettie’s household chores varied day to day. Sometimes she would clean the seven rooms of her apartment, or carry her clothes down two flights of stairs and put on a wash, or outside in the garden and tend to her tomatoes and basil. Sometimes she would be out there working in the dirt and watering, even when the temperatures rose to the nineties. One time during a New York City draught, Bob worried about Nettie working outdoors during a particularly brutal heat wave and made up a story that a policeman had rang the bell and threatened to give her a ticket if she didn't stop watering. Only that kind of threat could break her away from her garden. When she wasn't working on her garden, she could be found tending in Ann Marie's vast garden in Richmond Hill. She definitely inherited her love of the earth from her father, Cono.

When Bob woke up on a day that they would be going out, he would be ready by late morning, and the two would usually head to Ann Marie's in Richmond Hill, on the days when they didn't have doctor's appointments, to see their only grandchild. Or, perhaps it would be a day that Ann Marie would be bringing Peter there to spend the day with his Nana and Grandpa.

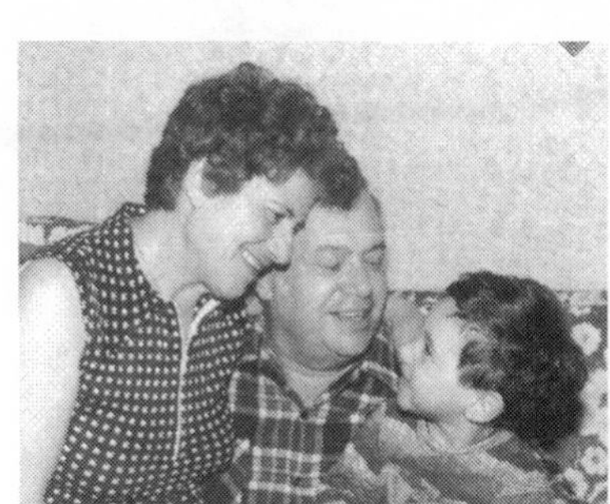

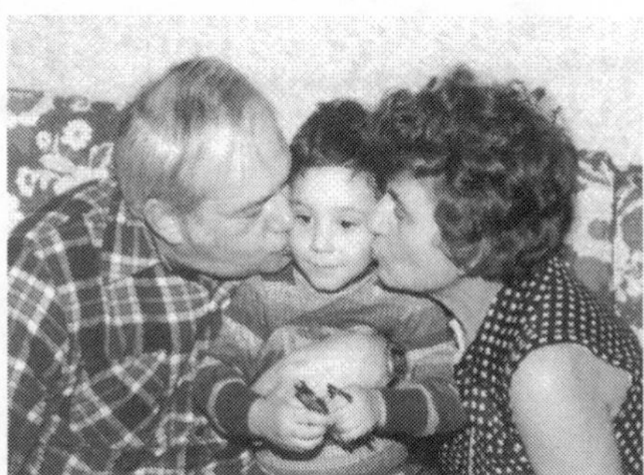

Nettie and Bob share a tender moment with their grandson

"Is it possible to love your grandchildren too much?" is the question that Bob Boniface asked after becoming a grandfather on

June 5, 1978. When I think of Grandpa Bob, I see a little boy running up a flight of stairs as fast as he could to burst through the front door of the Kingsland Avenue second floor apartment. Nana Nettie would be in the kitchen cooking some fabulous meal, the aroma wafting from the kitchen into the hallway before you even entered the apartment. Her arms were always outstretched to receive me followed by a kiss and her proclamation "Bello figlio del mama," beautiful son of the mother. "My prince is here!" After greeting my Nana, I would go through the kitchen and into the parlor through the dining room. There Grandpa would be, clad in an undershirt and pajama bottoms watching television either on the couch or his brown, Lazy Boy reclining chair. He would always give me machine gun kisses while enfolding me into his great loving arms.

Nettie proudly looks on at her grandson, Peter

Nana always called me her prince. "Mommy loved her first grandson beyond belief. He could do no wrong, not that he ever did! She was so proud of him," Susan said.

Whenever a button fell off of my Paddington Bear or the seams of the honey colored bear I had proclaimed his wife, Mrs. Bear, came apart, Nana would always have needle and thread in had and perform the necessary stitch to make my stuffed toy good as new. Most weekends of my childhood I spent at Kingsland Avenue. Grandpa and Nana would pick me up on a Friday afternoon and whisk me away from my Richmond Hill home to my favorite place in the world, 145 Kingsland Avenue. These visits began on July 29, 1978, even before I was two months old.

"Peter was the apple of her eye," Susan said in the summer of 2004, "he could do no wrong. She loved having him sleep over. She loved showing him off and bringing him to church so all could see him with her. I remember her carrying around a 'Nana's book' with all his pictures in it. I know she was so proud of him when he'd sit on the block with her and talk with her friends."

Grandpa was always a late riser, because he always had to watch the late, late, late show that went off many hours after everyone went to bed. I believe he got up sometime between ten and eleven every morning. By that time, Nana had been up for many hours, had washed clothes, gone to church, and was either done or half done with cleaning the house, in addition to taking care of her sister, Aunt Rosie, downstairs. There was also light shopping somewhere in there. When Nana brought Grandpa his coffee as he sat in his reclining chair, I always got a sip, as did my Paddington Bear.

Sometimes in the late morning or very early afternoon, Nana would get her little metal shopping cart from the hall and say she was heading for the A&P on Driggs Avenue, across from Winthrop Park. On hot summer days, we would welcome walking on Driggs, since it was a tree lined street; it was rare to find protection from the scorching sun during the summer in Greenpoint.

Nana was always a very busy person with a great deal of responsibilities on her shoulders. While she was not a person who would sit down and play games, joining her on her outings to church and the supermarket were always a treat. You never came home without some sort of item, whether it was ice cream pops with my favorite superhero's face, or the cereal box that had a highly coveted toy inside. I am sure that Nana was stuck with more boxes of cereal that she did not eat than I care to admit to.

When I wasn't with Nana and Grandpa, I was downstairs in Aunt Rosie's apartment. Aunt Rosie was about seventy five when I became a constant visitor in her apartment. After I arrived at Kingsland Avenue and greeted my grandparents, I would be in Aunt Rosie's apartment, where we would sit and chat-she would tell me stories going back to the 1910s. Always a very devout Catholic, she led a very prayerful life, along with her cousin, Flo DiCandia, who had been a postulate of the Dominican Sisters of Amityville in 1933, until she was forced to leave the mother house to care for her sick mother. Together, the two cousins, both never marrying, were members of the Third Order of St. Francis of Assisi in Manhattan and devoted their lives to God and teaching catechism to their families.

Sitting by the large windows in Aunt Rosie's bedroom, she would tell stories from the lives of the saints or teach prayers, devotions to the Sacred Heart and Blessed Mother. When she wasn't teaching catechism, she would tell stories of her childhood and about the Carrano family. The story of her sister, Carmela, who died from meningitis at the age of ten, was a favorite story of hers. Carmela's story usually was mixed in with the lives of the saints. And her picture, along with her mother, Maria's, were with the saints on the top of her chest of drawers, which she called her altar, which also held a large statue of the Sacred Heart and other smaller statues. Whenever Aunt Rosie had a special intention, or a member of the family was ill, she would light candles in front of the statues and pray for their returned health or the answer to her petition.

Rosie (left) with Nettie and Bob on Christmas 1979

When Aunt Rosie wasn't telling stories or teaching prayers, she would take you to her dining room table and play card games and dice. Grandpa used to tease that at Aunt Rosie's table; you learned "prayers and craps." While Aunt Rosie was a small, quiet woman in nature, her favorite pastime, besides praying, was singing. As she walked through the rooms of her apartment, you always heard her voice singing a mix of church songs with songs from her childhood and early adulthood. *Till We Meet Again, Daily, Daily Sing To Mary, Obey Your Mother Children, Just A Gigolo, Oh, How I Miss You Tonight, Let Me Call You Sweetheart, All Alone By The Telephone, I'm Forever Blowing Bubbles*, and especially *Silent Night*. Perhaps because her birthday was December eleventh, so close to Christmas, she lived for Christmas and Christmas carols. But of all the Christmas carols, that was her all-time favorite-she sang it all year long. The list of the songs Aunt Rosie sang could go on and on. Christmas always brings her to mind because you felt like she spent the entire year preparing for it.

While Grandpa sat in his brown Lazy Boy reclining chair watching television and Nana cooked dinner for the family, where the heat would be stifling, the window fan she had in there was largely ineffective. She had a curtain separating the kitchen from the rest of the apartment, which was air conditioned, due to Grandpa Bob's heart condition. I would spend time playing games, singing, praying, or listening to Aunt Rosie's stories until we would listen for the stomping of Nana's foot on the dining room floor, which was above Aunt Rosie's dining room. That meant that dinner was ready and to come up and eat. I would take off almost flying up the stairs, whereas it would take Aunt Rosie longer due to her legs deteriorating and her walking getting slower and slower as the years wore on.

The five o'clock news would be on the television in the living room, but Grandpa would be at the head of the table closest to the living room. Nana had put on a plastic table cloth over the dining room table and hot plates were in the center. Around the table sat the plates, glasses, and forks, spoons and knives on top of the neatly folded napkins. The napkin holder sat on the ledge of the china closet in case you needed another one. Everyone would gather around the table, as Nana carried in the pots full of whatever meal she cooked and placed them on the hot plates. Then she would say "Okay, gang" and everyone knew that meant to take your places at the dinner table. Aunt Rosie would lead us all in saying grace, and dinner would begin. The pepper shaker would be shared by Grandpa Bob and Aunt Rosie, covering their roast beef or macaroni, or whatever the meal of the day was. Aunt Susan hated pepper, and because I liked and disliked whatever she did, I hated it too, claiming it made us sneeze. I didn't really know if it did or not, but because Aunt Susan said it, I had to have the same reaction.

Grandpa would generally lead dinner conversation, which could be basically about anything. He was a news buff, which he passed on to my mother and to me, so current events were always a topic that could be discussed. Neighborhood happenings or things going on in the family could be discussed too. What happened at work or how was your day on a scale of one to ten was one thing that Aunt Susan didn't look forward to per say. But when she would walk in from work, having taken the subway from Manhattan and walked home from Graham Avenue, Nana and Grandpa's eyes would light up because their baby was home. Of course, this was only on the days that Grandpa didn't meet her at the entrance of the subway on Graham Avenue, where he sometimes parked on the corner and waited for her, leaning on his 1982 Chevy Impala.

As fast as she doled out the food to everyone, Nana was already preoccupied with clearing the table. I wonder if she ever really enjoyed any of the meals she prepared. Grandpa would fold his arms over his plate so she wouldn't take it away. Then Mom and Aunt Susan would join Nana in the kitchen to wash the pots, plates, and everything and put them away. The plastic table cloth also had to be washed, folded, and put away. One time when I was very young I decided I wanted to help, so I pulled it off the table cloth, crumpled it into a ball, and stuffed it in the closet on the bottom of the china closet. Nana called up my mother on the telephone later that night laughing when they discovered how much I had "helped" them.

After everything was washed and put away, Nana would close all of the closets, hang up the drenched dish towel to dry, and once again take out her long handled black pot with white specks to boil water for evening coffee. The television, which was never off unless they weren't home, would have the six o'clock news winding down and the beginning of the evening line-up.

As the 1980s passed, Grandpa's health began to deteriorate. Although by the early 1980s, he was only in his early fifties, his visits to his medical doctor, Harry S. Jacob, were at an average of every three weeks. His sugar counts for his diabetes were high and the circulation in his legs was poor, which gave him a great deal of pain. Once Uncle Patty Carrano died in 1981, a big responsibility was lifted from Nana's shoulders.

"Mommy would visit Uncle Patty weekly since his initial stoke," Susan said. "She'd take home his dirty clothes and wash them and bring them back the following week. Daddy brought her all the time. I took her on occasion when Daddy wasn't feeling well. A large responsibility occurred when Uncle Patty used to be picked up from the nursing home on Friday and then brought back on Sunday, from when he had his stroke in 1966 until Daddy had his heart attack in 1972. That was a big stressor. Not only did Uncle Patty get taken care of, but then we'd get a house full of company. And who did a lot of the entertaining? Mommy. I never thought anything about that until now and I guess it annoys me. Why couldn't someone else have taken over? I don't know if she did it out of love or sense of duty or both."

Bob throws Peter into the leaves as Nettie looks on in 1980

Before his health deteriorated starting at the end of 1982, Grandpa Bob used to rake leaves in my back yard and toss me into the mound when they visited us in Richmond Hill. We would be laughing. I was only about two at the time. Grandpa Bob was also the type of grandpa that always took me to Burger King on Manhattan Avenue in Greenpoint. He also took me at least once a year for an outing to the movies, in the early years to the Sunrise Multiplex outside Green Acres Mall in Valley Stream. It was there that he took me to see *Return of the Jedi* in the spring of 1983 and then to Burger King to buy the collector's glass from the film. I can still see him walking down Manhattan Avenue in Greenpoint wearing his trench coat, a Jabba the Hutt with Princess Leia glass in each of his pockets, one for me and one for Aunt Susan.

As the fall of 1982 ushered in, I began preschool at St. Mary Gate of Heaven in Ozone Park, Queens, but many horrors were befalling Grandpa Bob and Nana at Kingsland Avenue. When my family took a trip to Lancaster, Pennsylvania at the end of August, Nana came with us alone. Grandpa was suffering with his leg. Then in October, he continued to suffer with his leg and Nana came down with pneumonia. Due to her illness, I wasn't allowed upstairs and had to stay with Aunt Rosie while my mother cooked for and cared for her parents. In spite of feeling ill, Nana would come to the top of the stairs and I would stand at the bottom. With a big smile on her face she would say "Hello baby!" and I would call back "Hi Nana!" We loved each other so much and the pain was so intense, as I wanted to run into her arms as I always did.

Nana recovered, but Grandpa's problems seemed to grow more horrific with each passing day. During a doctor's appointment, his toe had fallen off during an examination right in the office!

"When Daddy started with his leg trouble in mid year 1982, Mommy found it hard to accept that Daddy was so sick," Susan said. "His diabetes had caused poor circulation and when he stubbed his toe was the beginning of the end. He first went into the hospital for the foot trouble, came home, and then went back in to have the toes [amputated.] It was quite a hectic time for all of us and I tried as much as I could to help Mommy deal with everything. Those trips to Manhasset Hospital weren't pleasant by a long shot. We all hated the place. I remember taking a lot of time off from work. He came home from the hospital after the toe operation on the day before

Thanksgiving 1982. I don't remember celebrating Thanksgiving that year, but we probably did, I just don't remember. It wasn't like Mommy not to have the holiday especially since she became a Nana."

Following this horrific event, the doctor said that Grandpa's left leg needed to be amputated.

On January 26, 1983, Grandpa went into Manhasset Hospital, which was an annex of Long Island Jewish Medical Center. The night before his operation, we were all down in Aunt Rosie's apartment when we all got on the phone to wish him luck. "I am going to pray for you and light candles with Aunt Rosie," I proudly announced to him. After I finished speaking with Grandpa, Aunt Rosie took me into her bedroom, where on the chest of drawers stood her statue of the Sacred Heart. With holy candles assembled in front of the statue of Christ, Aunt Rosie struck a match and lit them one by one. We then got on our knees and looked up into the face of Christ, his face illuminated by the flickering flames from the candles. I joined her in prayers of Our Fathers and Hail Mary's and asking God to watch over Grandpa and let his operation be successful and for all to go well. In my heart I kept thinking of Saint Peregrine, known as the "Cancer Saint" who according to his life story in my book, *Picture Book of Saints*, was to have his leg amputated, but Christ came off the cross in his room the night before the surgery and touched his gangrenous leg, curing him. I prayed for Jesus to do the same for my grandfather, why would he do it for Saint Peregrine and not Grandpa?

On the morning of Monday, January 31, 1983, there was no miraculous cure and Grandpa's left leg was amputated just below the knee. My dad's father, Grandpa Sam Franzese, took Mom and me to see Grandpa after his surgery. My Grandpa Sam is over six feet tall, and I hid behind his legs to be snuck up to the hospital. Also in the room at the time were Nana, and Grandpa's sister, Aunt Julia and her husband, Uncle Eddie. Grandpa looked well enough to me, but I was also horrified and intrigued to know that under the sheet of the bed he laid in, his leg was no more.

Grandpa Sam Franzese brought Grandpa Bob home from the hospital on February sixth. I stood at the top of the stairs of Kingsland Avenue as I watched-so many emotions filling my little head-as my one grandpa carry the other grandpa through the door and up the long staircase. It wasn't until April twenty first that Grandpa was finally fitted for a prosthetic leg. "It was a happy day for Mommy in a strange sort of way," Susan said. "By Daddy getting his new prosthesis, maybe life would again be more normal. I guess it was on a certain level but there was no denying that Daddy was really still a sick man." Grandpa was fitted for a prosthetic leg and also had to start taking insulin shots for his diabetes, which had been the cause of the loss of his leg. After losing his leg, Grandpa had to heavily rely on Nana.

In January of 1983, when Grandpa lost his leg from diabetes, he never complained, never looked for sympathy, and never sat at home to feel sorry for himself. Although he walked with a prosthetic leg, he walked straight and tall with every stride, just as before. No matter how ill Grandpa Bob felt, he always greeted everyone with his charismatic smile and booming greeting, bursting with warmth and kindness. Whenever asked how he was feeling, he always replied that he was well. It baffled Nana, who knew how much Grandpa suffered. His reply was that telling the truth would only make him feel worse. Illness never kept him home, until his health rapidly declined, and he always came to our home to visit or pick me up from school and take me home to Kingsland Avenue.

"The beginning of 1983 was no better than how it had ended," Susan said. "Daddy had his leg amputated below the knee and I know this brought much sadness to Mommy. Her rock was gone. More and more she grew to realize that Daddy was really sick and she had to do things alone, or with me sometimes. She was very patient with him and took extra loving care. I started to actually look forward to the weekly visits to Key Food on Mc Guinness Boulevard to do the food shopping. We'd try to make it fun. Mommy and Daddy had always done the majority of shopping together, except for those quick runs Mommy used to take to the A&P. They were a good, no, great team. Mommy and I did okay, but I'm sure she missed going with Daddy."

If Nana's responsibilities were not enough already, Aunt Rosie started to show the first signs of dementia months after her seventy seventh birthday that same year. Always having been active and known to travel far distances by buses and trains or even on foot, Aunt Rosie had always been good with directions. Then, one day, she forgot how to get home from senior citizens. This meant that Nana now had to keep a close eye on Aunt Rosie and monitored what went on down on the floor below her, in addition to what was going on with her seriously ill husband. When it became evident that Nana could not handle the full time care of two sick people on two different floors of her home, as she neared seventy, she faced that she had to hire a home health care aid. The aid stayed with Aunt Rosie for eighth hours a day, arriving around breakfast time and leaving for dinner time. Not only did Nana have to take care of Grandpa, there were quite a number of days when she had to accompany him to his doctor's appointments in Nassau County, and they would be gone for a large portion of the day. Aunt Rosie really couldn't be left alone that long, so the aid took some of this burden off of her shoulders, although it was an obsession of hers that Aunt Rosie receive the best care, and did the caring herself where she felt the aid had failed.

While it may have felt at times that Kingsland Avenue was on the verge of collapse, they focused on their grandson as a beacon of light to bring pleasure in their lives.

Nettie, Bob, and Susan with Peter on his graduation day from preschool in 1983

When I graduated from St. Mary Gate of Heaven Preschool in Ozone Park, Queens on May 21, 1983, Nana and Grandpa, was now walking on his prosthetic leg with a cane, but straight as if it were his natural leg, attended and sat in the front row. They smiled and cheered as my class sang *Over the Rainbow*, and recited poems.

"How proud Nana was of her little boy being so big," Susan said. "In short, they both loved to visit Ann Marie's house especially after Peter was born. Having a grandson brought much excitement to the house. She'd love to hear Peter sing and see him act."

In August of 1984, we went on our first annual vacation with my grandparents. We went to Friar Tuck Inn in the Catskills. Nana and I went on the minibus that took you from your room to the main building quite a few times to see different sites and go different places. That was a special time she and I enjoyed together alone. We went to the Seafood Shanty for dinner, and when we went back to the main building, Nana was chosen from the audience for a make-over. She had to sit in front on the platform as the woman did a make-up demonstration on Nana.

On Sunday, October 7, 1984, Nana received a shocking phone call from her sister-in-law Rose that her brother Rocky had died in his sleep from heart failure at their Deer Park, Long Island home. He was sixty five years old. Nana had always been especially close to Rocky and Rosie. Besides the close bond she had with all of her siblings, Rocky was the closest in age of all her brothers to her, four years younger. She had worked with him at Bilt-Rite Baby Carriages for years, his wife Rose was Susan's godmother, and they had gone on many vacations together, along with their friends Laura and Nick Chiaino.

That Christmas, as had been a long tradition with Nettie, Rocky's family spent their first Christmas without Rocky with us at our home in Richmond Hill. His death was followed three months later by the death of another brother, Jimmy Carrano.

"Over the years, the brothers started to pass on and each of those deaths loosened the foundations of the Carrano family," James Abramo said. "In the mid-eighties, Uncle Bob's health really started to go bad and now Aunt Nettie had to care for and worry about him as well."

Another large blow to Nana around this time was during her sister, Anna's daily visits; she noticed that Anna's memory was rapidly fading. Anna had always been the one of the four sisters that had been a rock to Nana, the one of her three sisters she could always count on. In fact, Nana had always referred to Anna as her "right hand." As years were passing, Anna's misplacing of her pocket book became more serious as she started to fail to recognize family members that she saw nearly every day. As Aunt Anna's son James said, when "Aunt Anna started her journey to oblivion, Aunt Nettie lost her "right hand." It wasn't fair to Aunt Nettie or to Uncle Bob for that matter, but life seldom is fair."

The Carrano sisters: Nettie, Anna, Connie, and Rosie in 1985

Although his suffering was great, Grandpa never damned God or resented his painful existence. Instead, he rose with a smile on his face and thanked God for another day. When Grandpa Bob lived to see another holiday or another milestone in the lives of himself and his family members, he felt blessed to be there. On Christmas Day 1984 he said “I’m glad to be here, believe me.”

On April 29, 1985, Nana and Grandpa celebrated their thirty-fifth wedding anniversary. Since Grandpa’s health had been deteriorating over the past few years, my mother, Aunt Susan, and Uncle Anthony faced the reality that they didn’t know how many anniversaries their parents had left, so they decided to have a surprise party to mark the milestone. The only information that Grandpa Bob had was to go to the certain hall for a party. He wasn’t told any of the details. Nana had no idea of the plans whatsoever.

Nettie and Bob on their thirty fifth wedding anniversary in 1985

On April twenty seventh, we had our celebration at a hall in Greenpoint. Grandpa wore a chocolate colored suit and Nana wore a salmon colored dress. When they walked in, Grandpa was overcome by the crowd and Nana was reduced to tears from the shock of it all. So many faces of so many different people that had touched their lives over the decades were assembled before them in this room. Even her dearest cousins had traveled to be with them that day, such as Jennie and Rose Mary DeLuccio, Aggie Zambrotta, Flo and Conrad DiCandia, and Mary and Oscar Rath. Their dear friends Laura and Nick Chiaino were there as well, and they stood at the front of the hall at Nettie and Bob's side as a priest from St. Cecilia's renewed their wedding vows before their relatives and friends.

During the summer of 1985 we took two vacations with Nana and Grandpa. First we went to the Poconos to the Mount Airy Lodge resort. Then in July we went to Marie and Ted Mehrhof's in Pennsylvania. Nana and her dear niece, Marie, who used to call Nana her almost mother, were together once again. Marie and Ted made a trip in about twice a year to Brooklyn to visit Nana and Grandpa. In fact, every Saturday morning without fail, Marie would call Nana and talk about the happenings of each week.

Nettie with Peter on his First Holy Communion day in 1986

On May 10, 1986, I made my First Holy Communion at St. Benedict Joseph Labre Church in Richmond Hill. While my parents, Nana and Grandpa, Aunt Rosie (my unofficial catechism teacher), Aunt Sue, Grandpa Sam and Grandma Josie Franzese, and others looked on, I received the body of Christ on my tongue for the first time from Father Jurgensen.

Every Wednesday, I would have early dismissal from school due to religious education for public school children, and there at the curb in their 1982 salmon colored Chevy Impala, Nana and Grandpa would be there to pick me up with Mom. Rarely, if ever, did we head directly to Kingsland Avenue. Usually, there was a stop in Middle Village, Queens. There Grandpa would pull into the stone gate of St. John's Cemetery to pay homage at three stops. First we would stop at the Lanzetta family grave, where Anthony Lanzetta was laid to rest, along with his mother and father. Then we would stop in Section 20 at the Carrano family grave where Cono and Maria were buried along with Carmela. Then our last stop was in Section 24 where Grandpa and Nana Boniface were buried with Uncle Tuddie. Grandpa would tell stories of coming there with his mother, grandmother, and brother for picnics as a child, since his mother's brothers were buried there as well. He and his brother would play and run through the tomb stones together, as his mother and grandmother laid out a picnic lunch on the family plot. Nana would tell stories of her mother making journeys to the Carrano grave to visit Carmela, whose grave was unmarked until Maria's death in 1957. She would point out the different saints her mother had used as landmarks and look for the open space between two stones where she had laid her seventh child to rest. With the hope that I would visit their grave one day, as they had visited their family plots, Nana and Grandpa taught me the value of honoring and respecting our dead forefathers and foremothers. After our visit to the cemetery, Grandpa and Nana would always stop at Silver Barn, where they would shop and always get me a container of fruit punch that came in a container that resembled the pint size milk container. After our little shop, we would then head home to Kingsland Avenue.

The smell of the Newtown Creek and the booming sound the car made as it descended the exit ramp at the Meeker-Morgan Exit on the Brooklyn-Queens Expressway gave the signal that we were approaching home. The sight of 145 Kingsland Avenue and the steeple of Saint Cecilia's were always a welcoming site. One of us would get out of the car to open the lock on the gate and swing the doors open for Grandpa to pull into the yard, and under the green carport awning, which he had built in 1982 when he purchased his 1982 Chevy Impala. Then Grandpa would get out of the car, we would close and lock the gate doors, and walk around the corner to the front of the house. As cars sped around the corner from Meeker Avenue to Kingsland Avenue, Grandpa was constantly worried about my safety and was adamant that I not go around that corner alone. They we would go into the house and relax. It was usually around one thirty in the afternoon by time we got in. After watching their afternoon soap operas *One Life to Live* and *General Hospital*, Nana would begin to cook dinner and we would have dinner.

On July 4th, 1986, there was a great celebration taking place in New York Harbor for the one hundredth birthday celebration of the Statue of Liberty. At Kingsland Avenue, we had a barbecue in the backyard; Grandpa, Nana, Aunt Rosie, Uncle Anthony, my parents and I. While we were barbecuing, a family friend, Freddie, stopped by in the yard to say hello because he parked his car next door in the Formato's parking lot. Grandpa had told me to go down the basement and get Freddie a beer. I was really excited because Freddie was there, so I ran down the basement and got the glass bottle. As I ran up the steep steps from the basement to the backyard, I tripped over the top step and dropped the bottle, which shattered and set the yellow, foamy liquid running in different directions. The worst part was that a few seconds after the bottle hit the ground, I fell on top of it and the glass pierced right through my leg underneath the knee. Everyone came running over and were very upset. Mom, Dad, and Uncle Anthony got me up and put me in the car. I remember getting into the car and crying not because I got hurt, I wasn't in any pain. I was crying because I was watching Nana cry as I looked out the window and Aunt Rosie cry as she swept up the broken glass remnants of the beer bottle.

Mom, Dad, and Uncle Anthony brought me to St. John's Hospital in Queens, where I got stitches. As we sat in the waiting room, we watched all the festivities taking place on Liberty Island, including an appearance by President Reagan. I was really excited about the Statue of Liberty's birthday, even though I had never been there, but sorry that I had ruined everyone's Fourth of July.

After I received my stitches, we went back to Kingsland Avenue. By time we got back to the house, the sun was well on its way down. Aunt Susan came home with her boyfriend, Don, to a bunch of glum faces telling her that I had been rushed to the hospital. Everyone was back in the house by then. Grandpa had the television on and was watching the festivities on Liberty Island with Nana and Aunt Rosie.

After the sun had set and the sky took on its murky, inky color, Nana stood at the tall, heavy draped window of her dining room and looked across the city, beyond the Brooklyn-Queens Expressway, out to the brightly lit skyscrapers of the Manhattan skyline. Above them on this night, Nana watched with bittersweet attention as rockets whizzed into the air, bombs exploded in the sky in the shapes of roses and diamonds or bouquets of various shades of color. Decades and decades before, in her childhood, she had stood alongside her girlfriends Rosie and Sally Lanzetta making these holiday bombs at the shacks near their father's Elmont bungalow back in 1927. She had seen them set off the *batteria* of fireworks at the Our Lady of Mount Carmel feast in her childhood, as well as that of Our Lady of Snow and other carnivals in honor of neighborhood patron saints.

As the heavy smell of burnt gunpowder wafted in the window, her late husband and his family always came to mind. While the sights, sounds, and smells of Fourth of July always furnished her with an ocean of memories, the fear and tragedy were always present. These beautiful works of art that filled a night sky with a few seconds of amazing colors had also irrevocably changed her life so many years ago. On an afternoon at the end of May, these same works of art claimed the lives of her husband and father-in-law. As she peered across the sky, she was filled with an array of emotions, but she could nonetheless deny that fireworks were emblazoned in her very soul. As her family filled the living room, lined up on the couch watching the displays on the television set of Times Square and Liberty Island, she kept her eyes affixed on the sky above the Manhattan skyline. Aunt Rosie, who was now in her eighties, disabled, and walked in a slow shuffle, rushed to the window to see the wonders above the Manhattan skyline. Grandpa Bob laughed saying that for a woman who could no longer walk, she nearly took off his arm racing for the window. Nana proudly told us how a firework was made, reminiscing back to the times she spent in the firework shack, her father-in-law asking for any able hands to assist in their creation.

Although it was painful, I stood at the window beside Nana, throbbing pain shooting through my leg as I too watched the fireworks light up and illuminate the night sky above the city of New York. Seeing the flashes of light across Nana face, she told me that there was nothing like Fourth of July in New York. "No one does it like New York," she smiled.

Another event that Nana and I shared each year was the Feast of Our Lady of Mount Carmel and Saint Paulinus on North 8th and Havemeyer Streets. When Our Lady of Mount Carmel-the church where Nana was baptized-opened its door in 1887, the Italian immigrants in the area began having an annual festival in honor of the Madonna of Carmel's feast day of July sixteenth. The feast day of Saint Paulinus at the end of June also had a feast for the patron saint of Nola, Italy. That feast dances a *giglio* as a sign of penance and devotion. A *giglio,* which means lily in Italian, is a five-ton, five-story tall hand-built papier- mâché tower honoring St. Paulinus, Our Lady of Mount Carmel, and other saints, which is carried by roughly one hundred men, while also having a twelve piece band on its shoulders when they carry it. The *giglio* is carried as an act of faith and penance in honor of the heroic acts of sacrifice and valor displayed by the patron saint of Nola in 409 A.D. Both the feasts of Our Lady of Mount Carmel and Saint Paulinus continued until the outbreak of World War II, when at that time they were put on hold until the end of the war. Also in that time, the church of Our Lady of Mount Carmel was demolished to make way for the Brooklyn-Queens Expressway and the construction of the current church which opened in 1950. In 1954, the two feasts were resumed and in 1957 became a combined feast and a greatly honored tradition of Italian American residents of the Greenpoint-Williamsburg neighborhoods.

Nana had gone to the feast for her entire life. When she was a child, her father-in-law, Anthony Lanzetta, would set off the fireworks for the feast. Later on, she would bring my mother and Susan, and Grandpa even took films of the dancing of the *giglio*. My mother had spent her youth going every night to the feast, and now looked to pass on this family tradition to me. When we parked our car on Havemeyer Street, I would hold Nana's hand and smell the Zeppoles boiling in oil, and the spinning of wheels, people shooting water into the mouths of clowns to see who would pop the balloon first. People ate sausage and pepper sandwiches, standing under the *giglio* tower, people calling out to each other, hugging and welcoming old friends back to the neighborhood. On occasion, Nana would see friends that she knew from different places. Even people she had gone to school with at Public School 132 back in the twenties. In fact, one year we met an elderly woman that she introduced to me as her Aunt Josie. This woman was a sister-in-law of Nana's mother. I hadn't even known Nana had any living aunts!

After we walked through and stopped at the different booths, we always made our way up the concrete steps to the shrine. Here, the aura of holiness kept the noise out. We would hand money to a lady sitting at a table with a metal box in front of her and a line of candles. Nana would pick up the wooden stick from the can, carefully light one end from one of the lit candles, and light her candle. Then we would make our way to the statue of Our Lady of Mount Carmel. On her head was a jeweled crown that shimmers from the candlelight. The statue's glass eyes give the representation of Our Lady a lifelike countenance. As we knelt on the kneeler and stared into Our Lady of Mount Carmel's face, Nana and I would give her our intentions to deliver to her son for us. Also, Nana would always open her purse and hand the woman a few bills to pin to the statue of Our Lady as an offering, and in turn the lady would give Nana scapulars. After saying our prayers, Nana and I would browse the tables and look at the religious articles. Either my mother or Nana would always buy me something there. Mom bought me a plaque of Jesus playing baseball with a little boy one year, while Nana bought me a children's book of the life of Saint Anthony, her favorite saint.

After our visit to the shrine of Our Lady, we always made a visit to inside the church. In the side room there is a shrine with roughly fifty saint statues to pray to. They range from different Madonnas, to popular and well known saints, to village patrons, such as Teggiano's patron Saint Cono, whom had been Cono's namesake and favorite saint. We always made a point to say some prayers and light some of the red, plastic candles. As we left the feast, we would always buy a bag of Zeppoles to take home, in addition to a calzone for Grandpa, as the music and smells of the feast followed us home across Meeker Avenue to Kingsland.

Late in the summer of 1986, I became ill with a kidney infection. I had a very high fever of over 104 for a number of days, with lancing pains through my abdomen and my family feared for my life. My poor mother, distracted by my illness, had to take her road test on August twenty ninth, but Nana never left my bedside. I was eight at the time. Nana and Grandpa were constantly at my bedside and took my mother and me to my doctors' appointments. Nana was swimming with tears as she feared that I was going to die. One day I remember feeling very weak and laying in bed when Grandpa came to my bedside and said that he would die for me. Those words were emblazoned in my mind forever. My grandfather loved me so much; he would make the ultimate sacrifice for me. It took three and a half weeks to recover from my illness.

Due to my illness, I missed the first few days of third grade, and also, we had not been able to go on our annual vacation with my grandparents. In spite of having missed the first three days of school, my parents got permission from my teacher and principal to miss a week of school for our annual vacation. On Sunday, September twenty eighth, my parents and I headed for the Villa Roma resort in Calicoon, New York. On that Wednesday morning, we drove back to Greenpoint to pick up Nana and Grandpa to join us on our trip. I remember parking in front of the house and them coming out with their little suit cases. Their bags were very small, and although Nana was the woman of many changes and always looked lovely, they traveled very light. This is in contrast to my family who packs for the safari even for an overnight trip.

Nettie and Bob join Ann Marie, Peter Sr. and Peter Jr. on vacation at the Villa Roma resort in October 1986

After settling in our time share unit, Nana and I went to the front of the building to wait for the mini bus to take us to the main building. When she and I got on, she was shocked to find that Nick Chiaino's sister, Flo, and her husband, Artie, were on the bus. She was doubly shocked to hear from them that Laura and Nick were vacationing there at the Villa Roma the same week as well. Nana and Grandpa were overjoyed because it had been many years since they had gone on vacation with Laura and Nick, since Grandpa had become ill. Laura would stop by our room every morning and bring Nana a cup of coffee. Then in the evenings we would meet in the dining room, where events were held such as Caesar's night, an Italian feast presented by a toga-clad service staff and featuring live music. Nana and Grandpa enjoyed that especially. As the trees in the Catskills turned from lush green to shades of gold, orange, and red, our vacation came to an end. We packed up the car, said goodbye to the Chiainos, and headed back to Brooklyn after breakfast on Sunday, October fifth.

CHAPTER NINE

TWILIGHT
1987-1989

"Trips to the doctors for my father and many, many prescription renewals were typical in 1987, which started out like other recent years," Susan said.

As 1987 rolled in and Grandpa Bob's sixtieth birthday approached, he faced yet another surgery. A bone inside of the stump of his leg had not been properly rounded during his 1983 surgery and was now causing him agonizing pain, to the point that he was not able to wear his prosthesis. Although Grandpa had led an active life over the past four years since his leg was amputated, this new pain was causing him to become a prisoner in his second floor apartment, leaving only for his doctor's appointments. His multiple times a week visits to my house came to an end, as well as picking me up from school on Wednesdays. In fact, even my sleeping over at Kingsland Avenue on weekends came to an end because he felt that he was no longer able to pick me up and bring me home. Although I still saw Grandpa and Nana every week, I saw much less of them than I had over the years.

On April twenty eighth, the day before his and Nana's thirty seventh wedding anniversary, Grandpa was admitted into Mary

Immaculate Hospital in Jamaica, Queens for the revision of his left leg stump. The aim of this operation was to repair the flaw from his last surgery and to return him to the normal, active life that he had been leading up until this point. He was released from the hospital on May sixth. Weakened by the operation, he was unable to get himself up the flight of stairs to his apartment. Nana picked up the phone and called Grandpa's old firehouse, Engine Company 229 Ladder Company 146 on Richardson Street for help. A group of Grandpa's fireman brothers came to the house and willingly and lovingly carried him up the stairs to his apartment. Although it hurt Grandpa's pride to be in such a vulnerable state, he was grateful to the fireman that had come to his aid, some of them who remembered him from when he worked in that firehouse.

On May seventeenth, Grandpa celebrated his sixtieth birthday, but due to his surgery, which had not even begun to heal yet, we had a quiet celebration at Kingsland Avenue. A few weeks later, we celebrated my ninth birthday up in my grandparents' apartment, since my grandfather couldn't leave it.

Bob with Peter on July 4, 1987

On the Fourth of July, we had a barbecue in the backyard of Kingsland Avenue, as we had the year before. Due to the fact that Grandpa's leg still had not healed, he came down the stairs in a sitting position, and we put him in a wheelchair and wheeled him around the corner into the backyard. Again, Nana, Aunt Rosie, Aunt Susan, Don, and Uncle Anthony were there, in addition to cousins Flo and Conrad DiCandia, who were visiting for a few days from Staten Island.

With a small television on the table for Grandpa to watch, he sat in his wheelchair underneath the awning in the backyard as we barbecued. Luckily, it was a quiet family day this year, unlike the previous year when I was rushed to the hospital. In the evening, the one hundredth annual Our Lady of Mount Carmel feast was going on, but unfortunately, Nana was not able to come with us this year.

Grandpa was too ill to be left alone, so Flo and Conrad joined my parents and me instead. To keep up tradition, we brought home a bag of Zeppoles once again and a calzone for Grandpa.

A few days later, Nana and my parents had to attend the wake of a family friend, and I stayed and "Grandpa-sat." Grandpa seemed very anxious that Nana was leaving him, but I tried to assure him it would be okay in her absence. Everything seemed to irritate him lately, why did she have to go to so many wakes and why did she have to put up all of her brothers' pictures on the china closet glass when they died. Was she going to put his picture up there when he died? That is what he wanted to know. His confinement to his apartment, the pain from the gaping wound in his leg that refused to heal, and the steady decline of his health with each passing day had him frustrated and scared. As we sat in the living room that afternoon, he in his reclining chair and I on the couch, the television going as always, he looked at me and began telling me stories from his childhood. I had not really known much about his childhood, except that his family moved a great deal, he was a latch-key kid, and his mother beat him mercilessly because he was inquisitive and found his way into mischief. The one thing he did admire his mother for was that she always wanted to know who his friends were and where he was going. Most of his childhood outings had been to the movies and to the opera. Then he looked into my face with a great deal of sadness as he told me a story about when he was about my age. He had gone with his friend to a pier somewhere. I don't know where it was, somewhere in Brooklyn. They were taking turns jumping off of it into the water. Then on one of his friend's jumps, he didn't come back to the surface. Grandpa tried desperately to find him, but was not able to. It wasn't until much later that day that his mother came home to tell him that the body of his friend had been found. The story had been one he had never told before and had obviously been haunting him for fifty years, of the friend that he had gone swimming with that never made it back to the surface.

"Around July eighteenth, my father took a real bad turn," Susan said. "He couldn't breathe and I remember my mother asking me to call Doctor Jacob, who said we should double his water pills, and if that didn't work, then he'd need to be hospitalized. The doctor mentioned that the increase should really make a difference. But sadly to say, by mid week, my father was still full of water."

On July twenty third, my parents, Nana, and I took Grandpa to his doctor's appointment at Doctor Jacob's office in New Hyde Park, Long Island. I waited with my parents for what seemed like an eternity, staring at the wooden door and looking through the glass reception window for a sign of what was happening on the other side of the door. When Grandpa in his wheelchair pushed by Nana came through the door, both he and Nana were visibly shaken. He announced to us that Dr. Jacob had found that his lungs were filled with fluid and that he needed to be hospitalized. Nana started to weep and tears filled Grandpa's eyes, and I began to cry and hug them both while standing in the waiting room. During the ride home, Grandpa Bob was so nervous. I remember him filling out forms with his name and age, and noticed that his once perfect penmanship was now visibly shaky. I had a pillow in my lap for him to rest his stump on. I was wedged in the back seat between my large grandpa and little Nana.

Two days later, on July twenty fifth, unable to wear his prosthetic leg, his breathing impaired from the fluid on his lungs, and literally sapped of all his physical energy, my grandfather slowly descended the flight of stairs from a sitting position. Sweat poured down his face and his breathing became heavier as a blazing July sun cooked the concrete stoop and cause the stifling hallway to become like an oven. He never damned God for this horrific predicament, but quietly suffered as my father guided him down the stairs. I stood at the bottom of the stairs, holding onto the banister with Aunt Rosie and her home health aid, Ida, at my side. My mother and Nana were also in the hallway, but Mom took Nana to the car so she wouldn't become overcome by the spectacle. Tears rolled down Aunt Rosie's and Ida's cheeks as they watched a scene that resembled the *Passion of Christ*. As he left the house that afternoon, Grandpa told my mother "I don't want to scare Peter, but I want you to tell him how much I loved him." Then, my mother said, "He looked at the house forlornly, trying to take in his surroundings as if for the last time." Then the four of them were off to Saint Francis Hospital in Roslyn, as I stayed with Aunt Rosie and Ida.

"My father had a procedure done where a tube was put down into his chest," Susan said. "When I went to visit him on Sunday morning, I remember him looking okay. We had a pleasant visit and he wished me well. I visited him early in the day because I was going out of town on business for the first time. I was going to Cambridge, Massachusetts. My mother didn't even come with me for the visit. I think I wanted to do it alone on that dreary, rainy morning. I hated leaving Mommy and Daddy that week though. Of all weeks the company had to send me away! I worried about Mommy being alone and I worried about Daddy being so sick. I'd call home everyday to hear Mommy say Daddy's okay. She never let on to me that he got really sick about mid week."

In the middle of the week, I picked up the phone one night to hear Grandpa-his voice filled with fright and confusion-wanting to speak to my mother desperately. He said that a doctor had come into his room and had discussed the possibility of having to remove his other leg as well. He was so overcome with shock and horror, and being helplessly in bed in the hospital, he didn't know what to do. My mother calmed him down and promised to call the doctor he had asked her to call. She was visibly upset though. Grandpa's health was not rebounding as Doctor Jacob and everyone had hoped, and Susan being so far from home, led the family to protect her as well as possible, until she was due home towards the end of the week.

"Mommy sounded chipper to me, although I detected concern in her tone over the phone," Susan said. "She didn't want to worry me while I was away at school. But I'm sure she wished I were home. Well, when I did arrive home on Friday afternoon, Mommy was thrilled to see me. She still didn't tell me about how Daddy had gotten so sick during the week. She was glad I was going to see him that night. I grew impatient to see Daddy, but I waited for Don to get home from work, and after we ate a quick bite, we immediately left for the hospital. Daddy was in intensive care where visiting was not permitted all of the time. When we got there, the clerk downstairs told us we couldn't go up because it was not visiting hours. Don told her that I had been away for a week and was really anxious to see my father and he really missed me. The lady listened to his story and called up to the nurse's desk and they told us we could go right up. Don visited for a few minutes, but then left Daddy and me alone so we could visit quietly. Daddy looked so remarkably well. Better than he had in a long time. He didn't look so thin. It was hard to believe that looking at him right there that he was so sick. Well we talked about my trip and I told him that I had visited with his friends, the Gallos, and they sent their love. He and Mommy were so proud of me, their baby, with AT&T and now traveling for them. It was such a wonderful visit. The nurses even allowed me to stay longer. So we were there earlier than we should have been and left later than we should have. As our visit ended, I told Daddy that I loved him, and as Don and I walked out the door, I turned around and gave Daddy the hand signal with the finger on the nose that we used to say 'I love you.' He returned my response in his hand signal with pointing finger to the nose and then two fingers held up, 'I love you too.' We smiled at each other ear to ear and I left quite happy. When I got home, I told Mommy that Daddy looked so good and that we had such a nice visit. She was happy and content that I was home."

As I sat eating cereal and watching Saturday morning cartoons on ABC the morning of August first, Mom handed me the telephone receiver to talk with Grandpa. The last conversation we had was a few days before and he had been so upset and confused. This morning when I spoke to him and chatted away, he barely responded to me. It was so odd to me; Grandpa always had so much to say to me. I don't remember what I discussed with him, but I just remember him replying "hmmm." I can't remember him saying a single word to me. Later on that Saturday, Uncle Anthony and Nana were going to see Grandpa.

"At that time, Anthony's car had been stolen and we were both using Daddy's car," Susan said. "So since I was there the night before, we figured it was better for them to go. They had their visit and I think they met Daddy's sister, Aunt Julie there. Anyway, when they got home, I went out. I spoke to Daddy about six that evening and he sounded confused. Something wasn't quite right, but I couldn't place my finger on it. Anthony was due into work that night. He was going to take public transportation to work, since as I said, his car was stolen and I was out. Then something overcame me at about eight o'clock I said to Don, 'hey, take a ride with me home and let's bring Anthony to work.' Normally when I left Don, I stayed home, but that night it was different, but I don't know why. I drove home, and that was strange too since Don always drove when we were together. We parked right in front and Don stayed in the car. I ran inside and said hello to Mom and Aunt Rosie, Mom was downstairs by Aunt Rosie. Then I went upstairs to tell Anthony that we'd take him to work. I don't remember if we called him first. Anyway, he and I were just about two steps down the stairs when the phone rang.

I ran upstairs and Anthony said he'd run down the basement to pick it up. It was Doctor Jacob and Anthony had gotten to the phone first and all I heard was your dad passed away. I said something like, what did you say? Doctor Jacob repeated 'your dad passed away.' I don't remember hanging up the phone, but I flew downstairs and ran into Aunt Rosie's house. I don't remember what I said or how I said it or if even Anthony said it. The next thing I remember is flying out the front door down the stoop to the car where Don was waiting. I remember almost falling down the steps. My father died, my father died is all I kept yelling. He couldn't get out of the car fast enough. We went inside and there was Mommy, crying hysterically and us consoling one another. She went screaming out the front door."

That night, my parents and I went to visit friends of theirs not far from our Richmond Hill home shortly after my mother spoke to Grandpa at seven that evening. At eight P.M., Grandpa Bob had spoken to his beloved Nettie to say goodnight. When he hung up, he turned his radio on and his earphones on his ears. Sometime right after that Grandpa went into cardiac arrest and doctors tried implanting a pace maker in his chest. Their work was futile. At 9:02 P.M., Robert Boniface was pronounced dead.

After Doctor Jacob called Kingsland Avenue to inform the family of Grandpa's passing, Nana's mind all but snapped. No, this couldn't happen again. Bob couldn't be dead! She took off out the front door and down the stoop and out onto Kingsland Avenue, screaming into the night that Bob was gone. Her neighbors for decades ran to their front doors and cried along with her. She wouldn't come in and wouldn't believe the cruel hand that she had been dealt. For the second time in her life, she was widowed. This time, she lost the love of her life. In spite of the many tragedies Nettie Boniface had faced so strongly over her lifetime, this was "the most devastating encounter of her life," my mother said.

"We tried calling Ann Marie's house, but this is probably the first and last time they ever went out without letting us know where they were or how to reach them," Susan said. "Uncle Charlie Abramo came over and kept Mommy and Aunt Rosie company. I'm sure all Mommy could think of was that she was alone and her refuge and rock was gone. In his heyday, there was nothing Daddy couldn't tackle. Well, Anthony, Don and I went over to Saint Francis Hospital. I don't remember if Anthony or Don drove, but it was quiet all the way there. We thought it best that Mommy didn't go. She was clutching her chest. When we got to the hospital, we couldn't see him right away. I guess they had to prepare his body. I was first to enter the room and he looked so peaceful. I laid my head on his right shoulder. I was sobbing, but it was so comforting to do that. When I lifted my head, Don and Anthony were in the room and my face was bloody. I panicked, where am I bleeding? This was my first thought. It turned out that Daddy had had a pacemaker just put in and the wound was still open, so when I pressed my head on him, I got his blood. We said prayers and then took his personal belongings and went home."

"Ann Marie, call your mother," my neighbor, Rose Garone called from a second story window of her home that faced our driveway. It was around one A.M.

Mom called Kingsland Avenue right away. Aunt Susan demanded to talk to my father. Then as I lay on our couch with the blue flowered design and my mother stood next to my father with the phone pressed to his ear, he said the words "Your father passed away." What emotions do you feel? I didn't feel any right away, I was paralyzed. Shock…grief…disbelief…fear.

As soon as we could get ready, the three of us piled into our 1981 blue station wagon and headed for Kingsland Avenue. The ride seemed like an eternity, but we finally did arrive there around two A.M. Everyone was huddled in Aunt Rosie's apartment: Nana, Aunt Susan, Don, Uncle Anthony, and Aunt Rosie. Everyone was crying. Aunt Rosie sat in her rocking chair in front of her china closet. She enveloped me into her waiting arms and said "Let Aunt Rosie love you."

Later that night, not long before morning, Nana and I went into her bedroom. Before she attempted to sleep, she walked over to her cherry wood dresser where Grandpa's fireman portrait and the portrait of her and Grandpa at my parents' wedding stood. Looking into his face she said, "Bob, tonight you're really gone." That night I slept on Grandpa's side of the bed so she wouldn't feel alone. Then just as we fell off to sleep, she said out loud in the darkness, "Dear Jesus, watch over us this night," as she did every night, and then the house fell into silence, except for the rumbling from the trucks on the Brooklyn-Queens Expressway a stone throw away from the Kingsland Avenue brownstone.

Sleep lasted only a few fitful hours, and the house was in full action at six A.M. Telephone calls had to be made, as well as funeral arrangements. By the afternoon, scores of relatives and friends arrived to comfort us in Aunt Rosie's apartment. People were around the dining room table or the kitchen, or standing, and some sitting on the couch in the living room. I sat on the couch in the parlor and was going to draw in a notebook to stay out of the way, but when I opened the notebook, the first page had a picture I had drawn of Grandpa. Then I started to cry. One of the visitors had come over to me to say that I shouldn't cry because I would upset Mommy and Nana and that I shouldn't draw any more pictures of Grandpa. I was even more devastated than before. Why shouldn't I cry? I had lost my hero; the world felt like it was coming to an end.

The next afternoon we walked into Evergreen Funeral Home on the corner of Nassau Avenue and McGuinness Boulevard. When Nana approached Grandpa's coffin she screamed and screamed, throwing herself onto Grandpa's lifeless body. My mother was at her side sobbing. I had not yet made it to the coffin. I stood by the chairs screaming "Grandpa, how am I going to live without you?" and cried uncontrollably. I buried my face in my hands and sat in one of the seats in the first row. My father took me out into the lobby hysterical, sitting me on a couch and giving me a cone shaped paper cup filled with water. Leslie Rago, the funeral director, knelt down to see if I was okay and talked with me. She took me into her office and talked with me for hours about the loss of my grandfather.

Grandpa was laid to rest in a wooden coffin. He wore the chocolate colored suit that he had worn on my First Holy Communion the year before. His body was cold and stiff, but he didn't look sick as he had the past few months. His face was not bathed with sweat; his skin no longer had the ghostly pallor. He no longer resembled the suffering man at the end of his ropes that suffered down the staircase in the stifling heat over a week before.

Grandpa Bob … as I looked into his eternally sleeping face I asked Aunt Susan how could we live without him? No one else in the world could give me machine gun kisses. And Nana, her eyes were affixed on him. She cried frequently, it seemed with every person that had come to pay their respects. At the close of the second night, I began to scream again. I was so afraid because I would never see Grandpa Bob again. My mother started to cry as we stood in front of Evergreen Funeral Home as she said, "You'll see him tomorrow," meaning for the funeral. Grandpa's trademark saying to me had always been, "Don't worry, everything is gonna be all right." How could it ever be all right ever again? One comfort was when we were coming out of the chapel one of the days, a jet was soaring through the sky above us, and Laura Chiaino said, "Look, Bob's going on vacation." We all smiled at that.

Time stops for no one, and the morning of August fifth came as fast as the rest had. The black limousine pulled in front of 145 Kingsland Avenue to pick us up for the funeral. We said our final goodbyes to Grandpa and all left his casket wailing, as we were led to the limousines. The shiny black limousine took us from the funeral home to Saint Cecilia's church for the 9:30 A.M. funeral mass. I walked behind my Nana as she walked behind the coffin, as Grandpa's "brothers," the current fireman at Engine Company 229 Ladder Company 146 in their dress uniforms, carried his coffin up the church steps and down the center aisle. I cried the whole way down the aisle, as I looked around at the packed church and saw so many familiar faces. Even Nick the Barber from Kingsland Avenue had closed his barber shop to attend the mass. Standing in the back of the church with a shopping bag holding the tools of his trade, Nick solemnly stood at the back of the church and bowed his head as the coffin went by.

With each gong from the bell tower of Saint Cecilia's, I felt a sword pierce my heart. I don't remember anything but crying. I don't remember how Nana reacted during the mass. I was too consumed with my own grief to take notice of anyone else's. Then after the rites of Christian Burial were concluded, Grandpa's Fireman Brothers once again picked up his coffin and carried him out of the church, as we all followed. Once he was placed back in the hearse and we in the limousines, our final destination was Calvary Cemetery.

Before we took Grandpa from Greenpoint for the last time, the hearse rolled down Kingsland Avenue, pausing briefly in front of 145, before continuing onto Calvary Cemetery.

During my many visits to the cemetery with Nana and Grandpa, we always went to Saint John's, but there were no graves available in the 1960s when they wanted to purchase a plot for themselves. Under the Brooklyn-Queens Expressway we entered the Woodside section of the cemetery-Division Two. The procession came to a halt on a mausoleum lined street. The pall bearers took Grandpa's casket and carried it between two of the mausoleums to his waiting open grave. When we left our cars, we were each handed a flower, as we too walked between the mausoleums, where Grandpa's wooden casket, now encased in a bronze colored metal vault, sat above the open grave. We crowded around the grave, Nana holding onto my arm. The priest said his final blessings, sprinkling the grave and casket with holy water. Following the prayers, we laid our flowers on the casket and each said our goodbyes. Holding onto my arm, Nana and I walked together back to the limousines.

After a dinner at Frost Restaurant, where a horseshoe of people lined the perimeter of the restaurant, a procession for the feast day of Our Lady of Snow passed the restaurant, as the statue of Our Lady was carried past the window where we sat. After the dinner was over, we all said our many goodbyes to the many people that had turned out for the wake and funeral. Then we went back to Kingsland Avenue with the feeling, now what?

"Mommy and I didn't talk alone about Daddy and how sad we were," Susan said. "I think she tried to shield me a bit. After the funeral, I tried to continue what I had been doing the last few months, paying the bills, making sure she and Aunt Rosie had their prescriptions filled and made doctor appointments. Mommy, I'm sure was glad that I picked up those habits from Daddy."

Following the funeral, the family decided that Nana shouldn't be left alone after the trauma of losing Grandpa, since both Aunt Susan and Uncle Anthony worked, so I volunteered to stay. Nana was very happy to have the company and smiled when I told her that I would be staying with her. From August fifth to August twenty second, I spent most, if not all, of my time with her at Kingsland Avenue. The house was much more noticeably quiet. It resembled how it was when she woke up every morning, only the noise never entered. Grandpa's booming voice no longer greeted us, nor was the television blaring in the living room as it had for so many years. In fact, the house seemed dark because except for the light coming through the large windows in the dining room and kitchen, the lights really weren't on.

While this should have been a time of reflection and emotional convalescence for Nana, family duties once again took precedence. On the day of Grandpa's funeral, Nana's cousin, Mary Carrano, who visited her and Aunt Rosie on a weekly basis, died from heart failure. Although Nana had told Aunt Rosie of Mary's death, Aunt Rosie continued to call her every day. And every day Mary's daughter would tell Aunt Rosie that Mary had died and Aunt Rosie would start crying hysterical. This would cause Nana a great deal of stress, as she would call Mary's daughter then and apologize, embarrassed for upsetting Mary's family at their time of death, although they didn't seem to mind. As the days were passing, Aunt Rosie's dementia was getting worse, as she started to think she was being attacked, tried to break a window with her shoe, and other bizarre actions. Nana was very, very upset over Aunt Rosie's bizarre new behavior and was never at ease, always worrying about what was going on downstairs.

On Saturday, August twenty second, Nana and Aunt Susan brought me home, after having spent about two weeks with Nana. School would be starting relatively shortly, so I was coming home to start getting ready. When we came home, Mom was sitting at the kitchen table making meatballs, but sitting at the edge of the chair because she said that she was having a very bad pain in her lower back.

The next morning we woke up to Mommy screaming on top of her lungs. The pain in her back had gotten so bad, that she couldn't move. She didn't even really speak, only screamed. Then, when Dad took her temperature, it was very high. Nana and Aunt Susan rushed over our house that morning. Nana was overcome by shock and worry as she saw her daughter lay there, screaming in agony. She felt totally helpless and was horrified because there was nothing that she could do to help her. The screams traveled to every corner of the house.

When the screams became too much for Nana to bear, she went with me to our neighbors' home two doors away, Frank and Rose Garone. They were getting ready for Sunday dinner with their daughter, Camille, and her husband, Jess. They insisted that we stay and Nana told them about the horrific happenings at my house. The Garones were always the most sympathetic of friends and Grandpa had given them the title of my "adopted grandparents."

When it began to get late and it seemed that my mother showed no improvement, Camille and Jess offered to drive Nana and I back to Kingsland Avenue. Although I was only home for a day I was back staying in Brooklyn with Nana. Aunt Susan stayed with my father and early the next morning, Mom was taken by ambulance to Long Island Jewish Medical Center in Queens. After a few days in the hospital, a nurse had put my mother in a chair and forgotten her there. When the nurse finally came back to put her back in bed, she was shocked to find the chair covered in blood and matter. There was a large hole in my mother's back, and finally the answer to her mysterious illness came to light-she had a cyst on her spine that burst right through the skin.

Nana's nerves were overwrought by this point. Her husband was dead, her daughter was seriously ill, and there was talk that she could die or be paralyzed, and her sister on the first floor was losing her mind to dementia rapidly. In spite of all this, Nana was very attentive to me, as we still went to church every morning, took our walks to the A&P, and spent time downstairs checking in on Aunt Rosie. At night we would sit outside in front of the Tropiano's house, where everyone would bring a folding chair to chat in a semicircle, having coffee at night together.

My father spent each day after work with my mother in the hospital. I would go with Nana to visit my mother on occasion as well. As August turned into September, Nana packed her things and came to stay with me in Richmond Hill, because school was beginning and I was entering the fourth grade. Nana preoccupied herself with tending to my house and spent most of her days in Mom's garden. My neighbors were worried about her because she spent so many hours in such high temperatures in the garden, not stopping to rest and cool down or get a drink. She was releasing her frustrations of having been hit with so much tragedy among the tomatoes and basil.

It was a Thursday night after school. Nana had made a pot of macaroni and sauce for her and me. Aunt Susan was coming to pick us up after dinner to bring Nana and I to the hospital to see my mother. After we ate and everything was washed and put away, Nana started complaining to me of a horrible stomach ache. We sat on my front stoop waiting for Aunt Susan, and as we waited, Nana grew more and more pale and rocked back and forth, moaning from her stomach cramps. Aunt Susan arrived and we got into the car and headed for the hospital. She was alarmed when she saw how ill Nana looked. "Let's not stay long tonight," Nana said to Aunt Susan when she arrived, "I don't feel good."

It was a fairly quiet ride to Long Island Jewish. Nana sat in the back seat because she didn't like to wear the seatbelt, while I sat in the front with Aunt Susan. We dropped Nana off at the main entrance and went to park the car in the garage. As we walked towards the main lobby, worry overtook Aunt Susan as said to me "I hope Nana didn't collapse in the lobby." We walked in and went upstairs to my mother's room. When we got there, she and Dad said that a nurse had seen Nana and said she needed to see a doctor.

"I rushed Mommy to Doctor Jacob's office, since I knew he was in, since it was Thursday and Thursday was his late night," Susan said. "When Doctor Jacob came out of the room, he pulled me over to the side to say your mom had a heart attack. I thought I was going to pass out. He must have seen this since I kind of slumped into the wall. He immediately had someone escort me to his office to sit down and compose myself. I don't think too much time lapsed and I ran back with her to the emergency room. I guess I called over to Ann Marie's phone in the hospital to tell them; I don't remember the rest of the night. All I know is that Mommy looked so sick and she tried to do too much. Her spirit and love said "yes" but her body said "whoa". This was God's way of slowing her down."

That night, Nana was immediately admitted and placed in the coronary care unit. I went to visit Nana once in the coronary care unit with Aunt Kitty, Nana's sister-in-law, while Nana's brother, Uncle John, visited with my mother and father. Nana looked pale and weak, but was very happy to see us. She seemed like her spirit was deflated; now needing a physical convalescence in addition to an emotional one.

On September fifteenth, Nana celebrated her seventy third birthday in the hospital. By this time, she was out of the coronary care unit and placed in a regular room, down the hall from my mother's room. In fact, she would take walks from her room and sit with my mother, with the heart monitor hanging around her neck. The nurses went to look for her when they saw no reading on their monitors, so she had to let them know where she was going in the future. On her birthday, we had a small party in her hospital room. We brought balloons, flowers, cards, and a birthday cake. My mother was wheeled on a bed into Nana's room for the makeshift celebration.

After a few days, Nana's room was changed to another floor, so she was no longer able to visit Mom. She seemed lonely that she was isolated, although Dad and anyone that visited split their time between her and Mom. I used to like to go and sit on the bed with Nana in her room. I wanted to be at her side through all the horrors that our family was facing that summer.

Nana was released from Long Island Jewish on September twentieth and Mom was released four days later, after having spent five weeks in the hospital.

"Mommy came home from the hospital on a Sunday morning and I remember her being happy, but not as happy as usual," Susan said. "Things were just never going to be the same. We tried to get some aid for her, like someone to clean the house, but after two visits or so we both agreed that was useless since I could do everything, since she would say that I had to clean the house before the aid got there. I did the shopping myself for awhile and that was okay, but we became a good team once she felt better. Mommy still tried to help out Ann Marie as best she could once they came home from the hospital, but she did have her limitations now."

When my mother, Ann Marie, came home from the hospital, she required a great deal of caring. She had not walked for five weeks and needed therapy to walk again. She also had a gaping wound in her back that needed tending to, and she had a visiting nurse and home health care aid come in for a few weeks after she returned home.

As 1987 came to an end, we celebrated Christmas as we had since my birth at home in Richmond Hill. Nana, Aunt Rosie, Aunt Susan, Don, and Uncle Anthony came over. While the absence of Grandpa and his strong presence was conspicuously noticeable, we felt very grateful for what we did have. Nana, although physically weakened by the heart attack, was still with us and slowly getting better; my mother had just about recovered from her illness and wound, back to cooking and was able to make a wonderful holiday for all of us as she always had. Aunt Rosie, although still sharing in our holidays, was only a shell of the person she used to be. After Nana's heart attack, Nana cancelled the day care for Aunt Rosie and got round the clock care for her instead. She finally came to accept that due to her poor health that she could no longer do all of the things for Aunt Rosie that she had done. Aunt Rosie's dementia was growing increasingly worse, especially at night when she would get night terrors, a sort of Sun Down Syndrome. As 1988 rolled in, Nana was also starting to realize that perhaps even the round the clock care wasn't enough.

Although Nana entered 1988 with a dark cloud of despair hanging over her, an early morning phone call in February gave her hope and anticipation that she had not experienced in a decade. After ten years, Ann Marie was pregnant again.

Susan, Nettie, and Ann Marie in 1988.

In March, Nana entered the New York Eye and Ear Infirm for a cataract operation with the hope of correcting her clouded vision, which was growing increasingly poor, in addition to the macular degeneration and "dry eye" that she suffered from. While she recovered from the surgery, her sister-in-law, Millie Carrano, Frank's widow, came to help Nana with her needs and to look after Aunt Rosie while she recovered. Unfortunately, the results of the supposedly simple surgery were disastrous. The operation did not heal properly, and the stitches that were supposed to dissolve did not, and had to be removed. For the rest of her life, Nana had to wear oversized, dark sunglasses to protect her eyes from sunlight, which is considered one of the causes of macular degeneration. Also, eye drops a few times a day became part of her regiment. For a woman who a year before was relatively healthy, Nana's health had taken a rapid decline over the last few months since her heart attack.

By the spring of 1988, Nana came to face that she could no longer take care of Aunt Rosie and had to place her in a nursing home.

"Mommy loved her sister dearly, but Aunt Rosie was just too much to handle," Susan said. "Even with the round the clock aides that came to live with Aunt Rosie, Mommy had the brunt of everything that went on downstairs. Aunt Rosie would scream at night and say we were all evil. Although Mommy knew Aunt Rosie was sick, hearing this had to devastate her. It got to me sometimes and I would get upset with Aunt Rosie myself. I was angrier with Aunt Rosie because I saw what she was doing to my mother. Mommy and I had discussions about nursing homes and the time had come. I remember telling Aunt Connie on the phone, Aunt Rosie is not going to kill my mother, so either you come here and live or give my mother some support in having Aunt Rosie go to a home. I was just so angry that night I hung up on her. It was one of the few times in my life I ever hung up on anyone. Mommy, I think, was surprised at my conversation, or lack thereof, but I think she was happy I did it, although she didn't like friction and she'd never go against any of her siblings, right or wrong."

On a night in the middle of June, Nana had my parents, Susan, and I spend Aunt Rosie's last night at Kingsland Avenue with her. She sat in the wooden rocking chair in front of her china closet with a New York Yankees cap on her head singing *Yankee Doodle Dandy*. Nana stepped away into the living room to weep, as she had to face the mental and physical disintegration of the sister who had been the angel of mercy and had helped raise her as a child. She also had to face her own considerable decline from the heart-attack that had irrevocably changed her life.

"Mommy didn't like slowing down and I think this was a big part of her depression," Susan said. "Yes, she did miss Daddy considerably, but she also realized that she could not do all the things she used to do, and at the pace she used to do them, and this disturbed her."

With the support of her children who fought any of her detractors in the process, Nana and Aunt Susan brought Aunt Rosie the following morning to the hospital for an evaluation to be entered into a nursing home. Nana demanded that she had to see Aunt Rosie every Sunday. "She wouldn't have it any other way," Susan said.

Over the summer of 1988, there was a great deal of talk in the news about the upcoming celebrations being planned for the fiftieth anniversary of the theatrical release of the film *Gone with the Wind* in 1989. I had never seen the film, but was curious about it because of all the news hype. After mentioning to my mother that I had an interest in seeing it, she urged that I call Nana and make plans to spend a weekend with her to see it. It was a weekend toward the end of August 1988, and Aunt Susan and Nana picked me up and brought me to Kingsland Avenue for the weekend, just as we had done so much only a few years before. That night after dinner, the hot air pop corn machine was popping, with a dishtowel over it so that the popcorn went right into the wooden bowl underneath it, and not all over the kitchen counter and floor. Aunt Susan got out the tape from Grandpa's vast VHS collection, and Nana and I sat on the couch, while Aunt Susan sat in Grandpa's Lazy Boy reclining chair. As the windswept title of *Gone with the Wind* swept across the screen, Nana had one of the largest smiles on her face I had seen since Grandpa died a year before. As Max Steiner's score filled the room and we watched the opening credits of the actors, Nana began to reminisce about the night that she had seen the film for the first time, back in 1939 with Aunt Connie and Uncle Tony, when she was a young widow at twenty five years old. Her eyes sparkled and memories of this film so dear to her heart filled her mind. For the first time I could remember in my life, she did not move, or have anything pending for her to do in the nearly four hours we sat and watched the film.

Since her health declined and she was finally relieved of the burden of the every day care of Aunt Rosie, after Aunt Rosie went into Holliswood Nursing Home in Queens in July of 1988, Nana became very reflective about her life. For the first time, Nana was sitting down and telling stories about her life, instead of in constant motion and always working at or involved in doing something. Nana and I would sit at her kitchen table and she would tell me stories from her youth. She would look back at choices she made in her youth and criticize them with the fifties years experience she had since then. She would tell the stories of Carmela, her big sister that had been so doting on her as a little girl, who had died so tragically at the age of ten. How much she idolized her brother, Frankie, from when she was a child. Or how she never would have left her first husband, Anthony's side if she knew he was going to die that night of the explosion. I sat and listened, fascinated by each story she told. She became more than just the Nana I adored, she became a heroine. She was a survivor and survived her tragedies as best as she could. She had suffered the pains of hell and overcame it all. She one time laughed and said that she was like Scarlett O'Hara. She had married her first husband because she felt that it was expected of her, and then he died shortly after, leaving her a young widow. Both she and Scarlett survived a war together as widows, and they both found dashing, handsome men after the war, and learned what love was really about. Perhaps, while they loved these men, they were preoccupied with other things that interfered with the men they loved. While for Scarlett it was an attraction to another man, for Nettie it was an obsession with the happenings and members of the Carrano family. While she was always a devoted wife and mother to her family, her brothers and sisters were always were in the mix of what she had to do. It was as if she never completely belonged to her husband, as a great part of her was always with her birth family. Then at the end, they both lost these men, Scarlett from abandonment and Nettie from sickness and death. Although Nettie loved and adored the "only man" she ever loved, she didn't realize the enormity of what she had until she lost it, as did Scarlett. She had fought so hard to save her Tara, 145 Kingsland Avenue, because it was the Carrano family homestead, accepting the grief her siblings would give her about purchasing it, because the love she had for the house outweighed it. In 1988, with her husband dead, and her sister in a nursing home, it was an empty house only full with memories.

On the morning of Thursday, October 20, 1988, Mom came into my room to tell me that this was the day she was going to have the baby. She and Dad dropped me off at St. Benny's, where I was now in fifth grade, and headed for Long Island Jewish, only this time for a happy occasion.

Rose and Frank Garone's daughter, Camille, picked me up from school that day and Nana was at my house cooking and both excited and anxious over the birth. Aunt Susan came over and Nana cooked macaroni, and in her old fashion, was taking away the plates as fast as she had laid them out. We had been waiting for my father to call us when the baby was delivered, but Nana said "C'mon, let's go to the hospital, I don't want to wait anymore." With a great deal of gusto, Nana had the dishes and pots washed in record speed, and in no time, she and I were in Aunt Susan's Buick LeSabre on our way to the hospital.

Nettie with Peter in 1988

When we came out of the elevator onto the maternity floor, Dad was in the hallway dressed in scrubs. "It's a boy," he announced with a grin, and Nana yelled out "I knew it! I knew it!" Many people thought that my mother was going to have a girl this time, but at 5:29 P.M., Dr. John DiIorio delivered a nine pound 21 ½" long baby, whom my parents named Robert James Franzese. Grandpa had always asked that if my mother had another son, that he be named after him. They gave him the middle name James in honor of Grandpa's father, James Boniface.

When Nana went to the glass window to see her newborn grandson, he was the largest and loudest baby in the nursery. He was screaming on top of his lungs, and it moved Nana so deeply, she went in a door and headed right for the container he was placed in. A nurse stopped her and said she was not allowed near the baby. “But I am his Nanny!” Nana exclaimed. Nanny or not, the nurse led Nana out of the room, much to her disappointment. Instead, she looked at her newborn grandson and grinned ear to ear saying how big he was. Then she looked at me and chuckled, “I have my Bob back.” We saw my mother being wheeled in the hallway and she waved to us. Her face was covered in red dots because she broke all of the blood vessels in her face during delivery. Nana went into recovery to see Mom, even though she wasn’t supposed to. “I am going to see my daughter,” she said in a commanding voice. She truly was our matriarch; no medical staff could keep her from her progeny.

That night, Nana, Aunt Susan, and I drove home to Kingsland Avenue on top of the world. Last year we had lost one Bob and this year we gained another. “October brought brightness back into her life,” Susan said. “When Robert was born, I saw Mommy light up again. That dimness was now lit. She was smiling ear to ear.”

The next morning, Nana and I went to church and in the afternoon went shopping at the A&P. Dad was coming in the afternoon to pick us up and bring us to the hospital to see Mom and meet Robert. When we got to Mom’s room, she was doing well, and a few minutes after our arrival, the nurse brought Robert into the room. I was overcome with joy; I was a big brother to this tiny baby in my arms. Nana took him into her arms very tenderly and fell in love with him immediately.

After our visit, Dad took Nana and I home to Richmond Hill. We weren't able to go back to the hospital that night because of a torrential rain storm. In fact, water started coming through the ceiling in the living room and the streets were flooding.

The next morning, Dad, Nana, and I went back to Long Island Jewish to take Mom and Robert home. When we went into the lobby, the guard stopped Nana and I and said only Dad could go up to take Mom home. "But I am the Nanny," Nana proclaimed once again, yet again it did not matter to the staff in this hospital. She went and sat with me on the chairs in the lobby, sulking that she couldn't go up. While she sat there though, she saw Dr. Badhey, the doctor that had taken care of Grandpa after his leg was removed. He had given her a warm welcome and chatted with her for a few minutes. She proudly told him that she had a new grandson. While he walked into the hospital, she made another attempt to get to the elevator to go upstairs to my mother's room. Once again, the security guard stopped her. Then she came up with a plan. She wanted me to go and talk to the security guard, ask him what time it was and what time the gift shop would be opening. Then, as I diverted his attention from her, she'd slip past him. Her plan worked because just as he turned around, Nana slipped into the elevator and the door closed. Nettie always got what she wanted.

I sat and waited for them to come down for what seemed like an eternity, but eventually Dad and Nana came down with Mommy in a wheelchair holding Robert. He went to get the car and the five of us got into the car, and brought Robert home for the first time. What a difference for my family with this birth, as opposed to mine. When my mother was released, she got to take her baby home with her. Also, instead of delivering early, Robert arrived two days after her due date of October eighteenth.

"When Robert came home, I remember Mommy sleeping over Ann Marie's house and being so excited about "baby" things again," Susan said. "She predicated from when he was a wee one that Robert was going to be a big boy. Mommy was happy, she had her Bob back."

Nana slept over as Robert spent his first night at home, and third night out of the womb. That night, Nana held Robert to her chest, relishing the experience of holding her new grandson. On a videotape recorded on the night that Robert came home from the hospital, Nana sat on the couch holding Robert to her chest and said "This is my little Robert. Thank you; he is a joy to all of us. It is an entire new life to all of us." With Robert's birth, there was a sort of shift in the relationship we had with Nana. We actually spent more time with her now than we ever did before. Although we only went to Kingsland Avenue on rare occasions now, Nana would spend a few days at our home every week. As 1988 drew to a close, we spent Christmas at home in Richmond Hill. This year we had a new addition and much to celebrate, as it was Robert's first Christmas. Nana, Aunt Susan, Don, and Uncle Anthony were with us. This year we also had another person missing from our table, Aunt Rosie, since she had gone into the nursing home six months before and was much too incapacitated to be taken out for the day.

Nettie, Peter, and Robert visit Rosie in the nursing home shortly after Christmas 1988

In the last hours of 1988, Nana and Uncle Anthony came over to ring in the new year of 1989. We sat around the dining room table playing the game *Pictionary*, a game where you draw clues to get your teammates to guess the secret word before time runs out. We played until midnight drew close, then crowded around the television set to count down the seconds of the dropping ball with Dick Clark in Times Square, as he declared the ushering in of the year 1989. After the New Year was proclaimed, hugs and kisses were exchanged by everyone, and the hope was that we would have another good year ahead. The year 1987 had been a nightmare at best, but the birth of Robert in 1988 had brought some sunshine back into the gloomy existence that so much tragedy had brought the year before. This would be our last New Year's in Richmond Hill, as our belongings were mostly packed and we were preparing to move into our new home in Deer Park, Long Island in the spring.

Nettie and Anthony (right) with Peter and Robert on Easter Sunday 1989

During the early months of 1989, my family and I continued to pack for our move to Deer Park. Nana visited our home constantly for days at a time as she got to spend time with her newborn grandson. On March twenty sixth, she spent Robert's first Easter with him. A few days later, she was back to care for me during a bad case of chicken pox. With the tender loving care that she always displayed, she sat at my bedside and attended to my needs. Later on in that month, she was very upset over the death of Lucille Ball from complications following heart surgery on April twenty sixth. Nana had enjoyed watching *I Love Lucy* for many years, and as she did with all of the monumental events she lived to see, she went to the grocery store the next morning to buy all of the newspapers reporting Lucy's death to save for posterity.

Three days later, on what would have been Nana and Grandpa's thirty ninth wedding anniversary, April 29, 1989, we finally moved from Richmond Hill to Deer Park, Long Island. That night, Nana arrived with her cousins Flo and Conrad DiCandia and her niece, Marie Mehrhof, and her husband, Ted, because they were all attending a party that night for her brother, Rocky's wife, Rose's seventieth birthday party in the neighborhood. In spite of only having moved in a few hours before she got there, Nana kept commenting on and complaining what a mess the house was because of all the boxes, in spite of Marie and Flo telling her that this is what happens when you move. Nana never moved more than a few blocks in her life, so she just couldn't relate.

After we had settled into our new home, which was pretty rapid since Nana didn't take kindly to disorderliness, she came to visit for a few days of every week. She enjoyed talking walks around the tree lined blocks in the summer, so different from Greenpoint. She also enjoyed visiting her sister-in-law Rose a few blocks away. In spite of her heart condition becoming increasingly worse, you would still find her on the front stoop or on the back patio sweeping.

She would also enjoy taking rides with my mother on Deer Park Avenue and marveled at the endless amount of stores, where she enjoyed shopping now that her ability to do so in Greenpoint was limited.

"Mom used to come over and we had a very bonding experience," my mother, Ann Marie, said. "There was no rushing to do anything, we watched T.V. together. I got to know and appreciate her for the first time in our lives. After she started to slow down, her children finally got to spend time with her."

Another part of her life that was different from any other was that due to her limited ability and weakening strength, she took the time to watch Robert's kiddy shows with him, and would laugh as she attempted to sing the theme songs from the shows to him. She enjoyed her relationship with her new grandson, relishing the experiences she shared with him as he made his new discoveries in the world. One summer day while she was sweeping, she found a small frog in the garden. She scooped it up in her hands and brought it over to Robert to show him his first frog.

Nana's presence in our home was always a great joy; in fact, I was devastated when she would leave us to go back to Brooklyn. I usually always tried to find a way for her to stay at least one more day. One particular time that summer, I had fallen off of my bike and received a pretty nasty gash around my elbow. I begged Nana to stay, insisting that no one could take care of my wound as good as she could, although I think my mother had taken offense to that statement.

Another much welcomed part of the days Nana spent in Deer Park would be her sharing stories of her life with us. As she spent more time sitting and reflecting, instead of in constant motion, she shared more of herself than before, instead of just sharing herself through cooking, cleaning, etc.

For my eleventh birthday, Mom had a family barbecue in the backyard. Since the barbecue was on a Sunday, and my actual birthday was on Monday, I begged Nana to stay for my "real" birthday. She could never refuse my requests for her to stay. It was almost like I had reverted back to the little boy that would cry when she and Grandpa went home with the hope that they would stay.

On August 30, 1989, Mom, Robert, and I spent a rare day visiting Nana at Kingsland Avenue. An early morning phone call came from Uncle Charlie Abramo, Aunt Anna's husband, for Nana. He told her that her baby brother, Johnny, had died that morning from cancer at the age of sixty four. After she hung up the phone, a shrieking wail came from Nana. She looked up at the ceiling and screamed "Mama, you've got all your boys!" A terrible sorry swept over her, as she saw the last of the six Carrano men go home to God. She sat at the red phone at the desk in the dining room and called her cousin, Aggie. Having lived through all of the agonies and ecstasies of her life with Aggie, she shared her latest heartbreak. Aggie answered the phone to Nana's sobs, as she cried that Johnny was gone, all of her brothers were gone. A short time later, Uncle Charlie arrived at Kingsland Avenue with Aunt Anna, now in the advanced stages of Alzheimer's disease. Uncle Charlie wanted Nana to be the one to break the news of Johnny's death to Aunt Anna, but the news seemed to have no effect. She did not remember she had a brother Johnny.

That afternoon, Nana went to Uncle Johnny's home to comfort his wife, Aunt Kitty. As she prepared to leave, she looked in her sliding door closet to retrieve a black blouse, slacks, and sweater, which she wore when she left. That night would be the first session of the wake.

When I arrived at the wake that night, Nana sat pale and somber, along with her sister, Connie. Anna was there also, but did not comprehend what was going on. Rosie was not there, nor would she be informed, now that she was in a nursing home and in poor mental health.

The following night, Nana was surprised to find that Aunt Anna and Uncle Charlie were not at the wake, and even more surprising, that they did not attend the funeral the day after. Unknown to Nana and the rest of the family, Aunt Anna's Alzheimer's condition had taken a drastic change the night that Uncle John died and caused her to act in a bizarre, uncharacteristic manner. Uncle Charlie, upset and not knowing what to do, called for an ambulance. She was taken to Woodhull Hospital in Brooklyn for observation. Unknown to her husband and son and obviously without their consent, Aunt Anna was then taken to Kings County Hospital a day or two later, where she received X-Rays of her head.

"I get to the hospital and my mother isn't in her room," Anna's son, James recalled. "I asked the nurse where she was and they tell me that she had been transferred to Kings County for some tests. When my father got there, he was really upset because we knew nothing about the transfer. He and I drove to Kings County and we eventually found her in the emergency room. She was laying on a gurney in the emergency room and looked like death warmed over."

A resident doctor approached James to go over his findings in the X-Rays of his mother's head. "He said the X-rays indicated that she had water on the brain and needed immediate surgery to correct the problem," James said. "Pressure on the brain was worsening her condition." According to the doctor, not treating the water on her brain would result in death.

James decided to bring his mother home and consult with her own doctor, who told him to admit her into Booth Memorial Medical Center in Flushing, Queens, under his care.

The next morning, Nana and Aunt Connie went to Aunt Anna and Uncle Charlie's apartment to help dress Aunt Anna for the hospital. "My mother was completely blank," James said, "she knew nothing or no body." Nana was overwrought with emotions as she saw her sister, whom she lovingly referred to as "Little Annie," because she only stood about 4' 10," prepare to leave her home for brain surgery. It broke Nana's heart that the sister she always called her "right hand" no longer even knew who she was.Although Aunt Anna's brain surgery was a success, the doctor told Uncle Charlie that she could no longer return home, she needed to be placed in a nursing home. After recovering from her brain surgery, and after careful selection, Uncle Charlie and James chose Bridgeview Nursing Home in Whitestone, Queens for her. Two of the four indomitable Carrano sisters were now in nursing homes.

As September rolled in, Nana faced her heart condition deteriorating with each month. The angina pains that would pang through her chest grew increasingly more intense and recurring. It seemed the nitroglycerine tabs under her tongue or the *Nitro-Dur* patches that she wore on her chest had little or no effect. Many nights she rocked back and forth with agonizing cries escaping from her throat.

Also in September, I entered the sixth grade and my teacher at the time assigned a writing project for us to write a story about a person we admired and looked up to. Nana came to my mind immediately. As her seventy fifth birthday approached that month, I thought it would be the tribute she deserved to look back at her life. When I came home from school on September seventh, she was so overwhelmed by the project that I had chosen for myself that she burst into tears.

It was a few hours past her usual bedtime. At this stage of her life, her energy was sapped as the sun melted away from the sky. But on this particular night, her heart refused to let her rest. The sharp pains of angina shot through her chest and made her let out moans of agony. No, the agony of her heart would not let her rest tonight. Through pain or rest, Nana never could spend idle time doing nothing at all. Although I was only eleven, I could feel her pain and suffering and it seared my heart to see her moan and witness the agony it put her through. We both rose from our beds and went into the kitchen. After turning on the fluorescent light, I sat with Nana at the dark wood kitchen table. She opened a drawer and grabbed a handful of rubber bands.

"When I was a little girl, we used to make rubber band balls. I'm going to make one for you," she said with a smile. Although the lines in her forehead revealed the agony that she was suffering as she sat there in the kitchen, her hands began swiftly working to create a rubber band ball for me to have.

As her fingers twisted the rubber bands into place, Nana decided to take the time to sit with the grandson that idolized her and share with him the information that he wished for so desperately … the stories of her life … the tales of his Brooklyn Nana.

Nettie at Marie and Ted's fortieth wedding anniversary in September 1989

On September 4, 1989, Nana's niece, Marie and her husband, Ted, celebrated their fortieth wedding anniversary in Pennsylvania. Nana and Aunt Susan drove out to Springfield that weekend for a surprise celebration given by their children. When Nana waited for the party to begin at Marie's daughter, Doreen's house, a fashionably dressed old woman with perfectly coiffed bright red hair came through the door leaning heavily on a cane. When this woman and Nana saw each other, they both gasped, and then hugged each other, dissolving into tears. Sixty years before, this old woman had been an almost mother to Nana. Nana had spent all of her waking hours at this woman's side on the second floor of the Beadel Street house. She had been her idol and been the one person that Nana could always turn to from when she was nine until she was fifteen. It was Marie's mother, Filomena. Up until her divorce from Frank Carrano in 1931, Filomena had been the mother that Nana had chosen for herself. Their divorce had been the first great blow in Nana's life, as she too felt like a child of a broken home, having lost her mother forever. Although Nana had seen Filomena over the years since the divorce on different occasions, she had not seen her since Filomena suffered a stroke at Antoinette's coffin in August of 1972. Nana said that although the stroke had severely impaired Filomena's speech, no words were needed that day. She said Filomena would get frustrated because there were so many things she wanted to say to her, but was unable to utter them. Nana held her hand and any hurts and disappointments that were harbored from so many years before vanished. Nana had finally made peace with her past with Filomena, which had always left a sort of brokenness in her from her childhood that she had never quite resolved. The ironic thing was that Filomena, then eighty four, had expressed a wish to her family to see Nana one more time before her death.

"When they were together, it was like no one else was around them," Marie Mehrhof said.

When Nana came home from the party, she stood in front of my stove and she looked at me. Tears began to fill her eyes and her voice cracked, although a smile was on her face. “I saw [Filomena,]” she said. “She was so happy to see me. How we cried! There were so many things she wanted to say to me, but she couldn’t, but I understood. I saw it in her eyes.” Nana finally found inner peace by an unspoken reconciliation with this woman she had loved so much in her past.

On September 15, 1989, Nettie Carrano Boniface turned seventy five. In addition to the chronicle of her life I was in the process of writing, I collected pictures taken of Nana during her lifetime and hung them over the entrance of our dining room with a banner “Happy 75th Birthday, Nana.” When Nana came over that weekend to celebrate her birthday, she cried as she saw the pictures beginning with her confirmation picture when she was about eight or nine years old, up to a picture taken the week before with Robert.

As the stories continued to be told, the class story had become a twenty page report chronicling twenty important events from Nana’s life, as she had told them to me. I finished her story by the end of September and was expected to begin work on the final draft to be presented by the third week of October.

In the midst of her life story being recorded for posterity and the celebration of her seventy fifth birthday, Nana’s failing health was always a constant issue she had to deal with. On September tenth, she was admitted into Saint Francis Hospital in Roslyn, the same hospital where Grandpa died, as an outpatient for two chest views, an EKG, and diagnostic tests. She was then scheduled to return there for an angiogram, since the cause of her heart problems was three blocked arteries in her heart. Aunt Susan took her to the hospital for both of these appointments, but unfortunately, the angiogram was not a success. During a nine A.M. appointment on October third with Dr. Hartstein, she was told that the only cure for her ailing heart was coronary bypass surgery.

Nettie and Robert in October 1989

After learning of the news that Nana's coronary bypass surgery was to take place on Robert's first birthday, October twentieth, Mom decided to hold the birthday celebration on October seventh so Nana could partake in the occasion. Although she could not pick Robert up due to her heart condition, she helped him tear into his gifts as they were opened one by one. At the end of the night though, she started to cry when she said goodbye to the guests. She was afraid she would never see them again. Laura and Nick Chiaino came by to see her, and comfort her, because they knew Nana was scared. They had stood by her through all of the joys and sorrows she faced for more than thirty years.

Aunt Susan was off for Columbus Day, October ninth, so Nana asked her to take her to see her two sisters that day. "She would never abandon her sisters no matter how sick she felt," Susan said. "We went to see Aunt Rosie and Aunt Anna in their nursing homes. She admitted to me afterwards that the two visits were too much for her in one day and she wouldn't be able to do that again."

On October fifteenth, Nana and Aunt Susan spent the day at our house in Deer Park. It would be Nana's last visit before the operation, although she would be staying at our home for an extended amount of time to recover. Mom had purchased a pull out bed for my bedroom, so Nana would have a bed to recover in. It would be arriving on October twenty third. All of the plans were made, when she was ready to be released from the hospital, her friends Laura and Nick Chiaino were going to pick her up and bring her to my house to recuperate. Mom would take care of her, since she didn't work, until Nana was able to be by herself at home. We wanted Nana to come live with us, but she would never leave her beloved 145 Kingsland Avenue behind.

While it seemed that coronary bypass surgery was common, there was always that possibility that Nana could die. This was the most frightening thing to me in the world. I remember seeing her sitting in my living room in the wooden rocking chair with a pale blue blouse and dark slacks, sitting there rocking and smiling. I had asked her to stay longer, but she was insistent that she had to go home, since later in the week she would be entering the hospital. I kept leaving the room and sitting on the floor of Robert's bedroom under the window, crying as silently as I could, so she wouldn't know or hear me.

Nettie with Peter and Robert on October 15, 1989, five days before her coronary bypass surgery

Before she left with Aunt Susan that day, Mommy took my Polaroid camera and snapped a few pictures of Nana sitting in the rocking chair holding Robert; I am standing next to them, Nana's head and mine are together.

During that week, unbeknownst to the family, Nana sat at the desk in the dining room, and thumbing through her worn blue phone book, picked up her red phone and made calls to say goodbye. "Mom had become an extremely lonely person, yet she would fight with you if you tried to get her to leave Kingsland Avenue," my mother said.

On Wednesday, October eighteenth, my mother let me stay home from school and she and I, along with Robert, were dropped off by Daddy at Kingsland Avenue to spend Nana's last day at Kingsland Avenue before her operation. Nana cooked that day like she always had, but did everything with a nervous gusto. Over the past few months, she had reflected on death and thought about her experiences with her loved ones that had died over the years. Her new saying to us was, "when I die, you'll miss me." Over the past month, she had talked of death often. She said to me one day that when she died, she promised to appear to me, but regardless if she could or not, she would let me know somehow that she was with me always. I told her that I thought when she died, she would be canonized a saint. She was so shocked and honored that she started to cry.

As we left that night to come home, Nana walked us into the hallway and stood at the top of the stairs as we made our way down to leave. I remember hugging and kissing her, then walking down the stairs. Then just before I went through the doorway, I turned around to look at her again. She stood there smiling at me, like as if she were at the top of the stairway to heaven. I wanted to run up the stairs and cry, begging her not to go for the operation, but I yelled one more goodbye to her and left. Before she went to bed that night, Nana turned to Aunt Susan and said, "what do you think Sue? Do you think I'll be ok?"

The next morning, Uncle Anthony drove Nana to Saint Francis Hospital in Roslyn for the surgery. He told her that if she changed her mind about the operation, he would turn the car around, but she said it was something she had to do. That day she was prepped, and when she called that night, she sounded upbeat and hopeful, but anxious. She mentioned that she had received last rites and was ready for the operation ahead. Before she went to bed that night, Nana set her hair with the little pink curlers that she had brought to the hospital. Even going in for heart surgery, Nettie Boniface never faced anything in life without perfectly coiffed hair. That night, Aunt Susan and Don visited Nana at the hospital, and she said to Susan one more time, "do you think I am doing the right thing?"

The following morning, Mom and Aunt Susan waited with Aunt Connie and Uncle Tony in the waiting room while Nana's surgery was underway. The triple bypass operation was more complicated than the surgeon realized. Her age, small stature, and a previously undetected leaking valve made the operation more difficult that previously anticipated. She did make it through the operation, and that night, Mom, Dad, and Aunt Susan saw her when she came out of recovery. Although her voice was very high pitched when she came out of the surgery, she was coherent and alert. Mom mentioned that Aunt Connie had been in the waiting room for the duration of the operation. Nana's eyes widened with shock. After she had placed Aunt Rosie in the nursing home, there had been a great strain put on her relationship with her sister, Connie, but the love the sisters had for one another always beat out any strains and hurts between them.

The following afternoon, Aunt Susan stopped at the hospital to see Nana. She complained that her feet were cold, so Aunt Susan took off her socks and put them on Nana. That made Nana happy. Later that evening, Aunt Susan returned to the hospital with Mom and Dad. They found her more alert and conversational. She mentioned that her niece, Doreen, would be getting married that day. She also asked the nurse if she could give the sandbag pillow with the heart character drawn on it that said "Nettie's huggie" to her grandson. But they told her that the pillow was needed to heal her chest. She complained of chest pain, and Mom said, "But Mom, you just had heart surgery, of course your chest hurts." Nana then asked if I was downstairs in the hospital lobby and could she see me, but I was at home doing my homework and not allowed in the hospital due to my age. That night, she had seemed to have had a big improvement, and when the three of them left the hospital, it was with relief that Nana was going to be all right.

After much urging by family and friends, Aunt Susan slept over our house that night. At 5 A.M. the telephone rang. Aunt Susan and I jumped out of bed to get it. It was the hospital, "your mother had taken a turn for the worse. We urge you to come to the hospital right away."

Susan ran into my mother's room, "Ann Marie, Mommy's bad, we have to get to the hospital right away."

"But she was doing so good," my mother replied.

Mom and Aunt Susan got dressed, called Uncle Anthony to meet them at the hospital, and left immediately. Dad had to wait behind for Grandpa Sam Franzese and Aunt Jennie to come to our house from Brooklyn to stay with us. He couldn't leave his one-year-old son with an eleven year old in the middle of the night. When Grandpa and Aunt Jennie arrived, he went to the hospital as well.

When Mom and Aunt Susan arrived at the hospital, they were immediately led up to the intensive care unit, where their mother was unconscious when they arrived. The doctor had told them that her heart had gone into shock, and that she had woken up and realized that she was dying, so they had put her under anesthesia. The nurses told them to talk to their mother, that although she was not conscious, she could hear them. After a few minutes with their mother, Nettie's three children went downstairs to the waiting room, awaiting news on their mother's fate. They called her sister, Connie, who rushed to the hospital with her husband, Tony, and son, Joseph. Before going for the operation, Nana said to my mother that she couldn't die because she had to be there for me, but her life was not to be.

The doctor finally came into the waiting room to address the group. "We did everything we could, but we lost her." At 8:40 A.M. on Sunday, October 22, 1989, Nettie Boniface was pronounced dead.

As the shock and horror ripped through the room, the assembly of Nettie's family was told that they could go upstairs to see her for the last time.

The crowd that included her three children, son-in-law, and sister, encircled Nettie's deathbed. She lay there in eternal rest, as her family cried and said goodbye one by one. "Nettie, you broke the chain of us sisters," Connie screamed, as she cried and kissed Nettie's face. Throughout the decades, it was the Carrano sisters that had stuck together. As James Abramo said, "never have I seen four sisters that cared for each other so much, or defended each other so much, or loved each other so much … Whatever hurt feelings or petty jealousies or ill will that passed between them on occasion was nothing, compared to the deep sisterly love that was there."

News of Nettie's death traveled quickly, much to the horror of anyone who received it. "I remember the morning my father telephoned me in New Jersey and told me that Aunt Nettie had died," James said. "He was stunned and in disbelief. He actually hung up on me saying, '… oh my God, Nettie has died."

"Nettie's death just sent me for a loop," Laura said. "I just couldn't believe it. It took a long time for me to get over it."

It was around eleven A.M. when my parents came through the door. My mother's face was tearstained and she held a large plastic bag in her hand. I asked her how Nana was doing. She sat down in the wooden rocking chair and replied, "Nana's with God." I threw myself into her arms and screamed. Then I ran into my parents' bedroom and threw myself on top of the bed. I wanted to die, I couldn't face the pain.

In a state of shock and disbelief, we packed clothes and headed for Brooklyn. Robert and I stayed with Grandpa Sam and Grandma Josephine while my parents attended to funeral arrangements. As I lay in bed that night, I buried my face into the pillow, "Nana is gone," I thought to myself, "the end of the era of Nettie Carrano Boniface," whose life I had so proudly written over the last month.

The following two afternoons and evenings, Nana's wake took place at Evergreen Funeral Home, the same place where Grandpa's wake had taken place two years before. When my parents and I arrived at the chapel on the first day, I saw Nana's name on the same door where Grandpa's wake had taken place. As we walked through the door, I saw a still, small figure lying in state in the distance. Uncle Anthony was at the coffin crying. I knelt with my mother at the coffin, looking into her face bewildered. How could Nana be dead? Her thick, beautiful brown hair was perfectly coiffed to her approval. Although her face looked serene, he neck was swollen from the heart surgery. Her hands were folded in prayer with the crystal rosary she brought with her to church each morning entwined through her fingers. She wore the turquoise, sequined gown she wore to my parents' wedding fourteen years before. The gown shimmered from the light given off by the dim lamps at the head and foot of the coffin. Little sky-blue slippers peaked from the bottom of the gown.

I put my face to hers and felt the cool stiffness that made me realize that Nana really was no longer of this world. There was no greeting for the prince, no "bello figlio del mama," no hugs or kisses. Shaken, I picked up one of the memorial cards on the small tray next to the coffin and read it: "In Loving Memory of Nettie Boniface, October 22, 1989." I ran from the room crying.

I sat where Nana had sat in the front row when Grandpa had died, getting up once in a while to stare into her face, fix her sleeve, or whisper some last things I needed to tell her. It amazed me that of the indomitable four Carrano sisters, only one was at her wake. Nana had two sisters on earth that not only were not at her wake, but would never know of her death. Connie was left to mourn the first of the legendary four to die alone.

At the ten A.M. funeral mass, Nana was eulogized by Father Michael Phillips, the pastor of Saint Cecilia's on Wednesday, October twenty fifth, as a mainstay of the church whose daily presence in the first pew, whose devotion had been an inspiration to her grandson and so many others, would be greatly missed. The aisle where she had walked down twice as a bride and widow was where her coffin was now carried. Her friends that joined her each morning at mass were in the pews to bid her farewell. I cried through the mass and caressed the coffin as I stood on line for Holy Communion. Then I sobbed as I walked behind her being carried out of St. Cecilia's-the church she had loved and supported for so many years-for the last time.

A large crowd stood around Nana's coffin next to her open grave at Calvary Cemetery, where Father Phillips blessed her eternal resting place, where her remains would be reunited with her beloved Bob's, reunited for eternity. I dropped a flower on her coffin, now encased in a bronze colored metal vault, and went back to the limousine. "When Nana died, we became adults," my father said. "When Mommy died, 145 Kingsland Avenue just became a house," my mother said.

When we went to pick up Robert from my grandparents home after the funeral, our tears dried pretty quickly. As we laid Nana to rest, Robert took his first steps.

Nettie and Bob's grave in Calvary Cemetery

CHAPTER TEN

FAREWELL
1996

Brooklyn-born chronicler of the great borough of her birth, Betty Smith, described seeing Greenpoint-Williamsburg for the last time as poignant as "death itself … oh, the last time how clearly you see everything; as though a magnifying light had been turned on it. And you grieve because you hadn't held it tighter when you had it every day."

I stood in Nana's bedroom one summer day in 1996 to say farewell to the house where the story of her life had taken place. I stood in front of the cherry wood dresser and looked at my reflection in the mirror. A photograph came to mind of my mother standing in the same place putting on her wedding veil twenty three years before. In the reflection of the photo, you can see my grandparents looking on from the corner of the room. Was I looking for them in that corner? I will never know. I was searching, but for a nameless purpose.

I pulled open the top left drawer. It was now devoid of the memorial cards from the scores of wakes Nana attended over the years. There were also no hair nets, kerchiefs, or handkerchiefs in sight. I walked over to the end table next to the bed and opened the top drawer. Nana's spare rosaries were not there, and I knew Grandpa's socks will not be in the top drawer of the other end table. What was I searching for in empty drawers? What was I hoping to find?

The door was about to permanently be closed on La Casa Carrano-145 Kingsland Avenue. In May, ten of Maria and Cono's thirteen grandchildren had come home, along with their only surviving child of their eleven children, to both celebrate and commemorate the ones who had gone before as we held a wake of a different kind, for the place we had all called home. As family members sat in the living room and dining room, Bette Midler's *Wind Beneath My Wings* and Billy Joel's *This Is The Time* filled the rooms, as photographs of the family flashed across the television screen. Aunt Connie, at seventy nine, the sole survivor of the eleven children, sat in a rocking chair and let out sobs as she remembered her parents and the siblings she had buried one by one. "I had a beautiful family. Too bad they're all gone," she said. Aunt Anna had died from Alzheimer's disease in 1992 a month before her eighty second birthday. Aunt Rosie spent six years in Holliswood nursing home, where she was wheelchair bound and semi-aware from the advanced stages of dementia. Aunt Susan kept her promise to her mother to "never forget my sister" and visited Aunt Rosie frequently. I had joined her many times over the years and always brought pictures of the family to keep her memory intact. On her eighty eighth birthday, December 11, 1993, Aunt Rosie looked at Nana and Grandpa's picture and said "I know they're gone." What made her say this, I will never know. She then said “thank you for not forgetting me.” A month later, she somehow broke her left leg. When the cast was removed in May, the leg was gangrenous and had to be removed. A short time later, she lapsed into a coma, and died on the anniversary of Nana’s eightieth birthday, September 15, 1994, less than three months before her eighty ninth birthday. I feel pretty certain it was Nana who came to bring her sister to the Kingsland Avenue in the sky.

Peter and Rosie on her eighty eighth birthday in December 1993. She died nine months later on Nettie’s eightieth birthday.

Tears were shed and memories shared before the cousins all gathered in the living room for a final photo. Aunt Connie made the stairs forlornly, leaving the house for the last time that had given her strength, as she said when her husband, Tony, died in 1992.

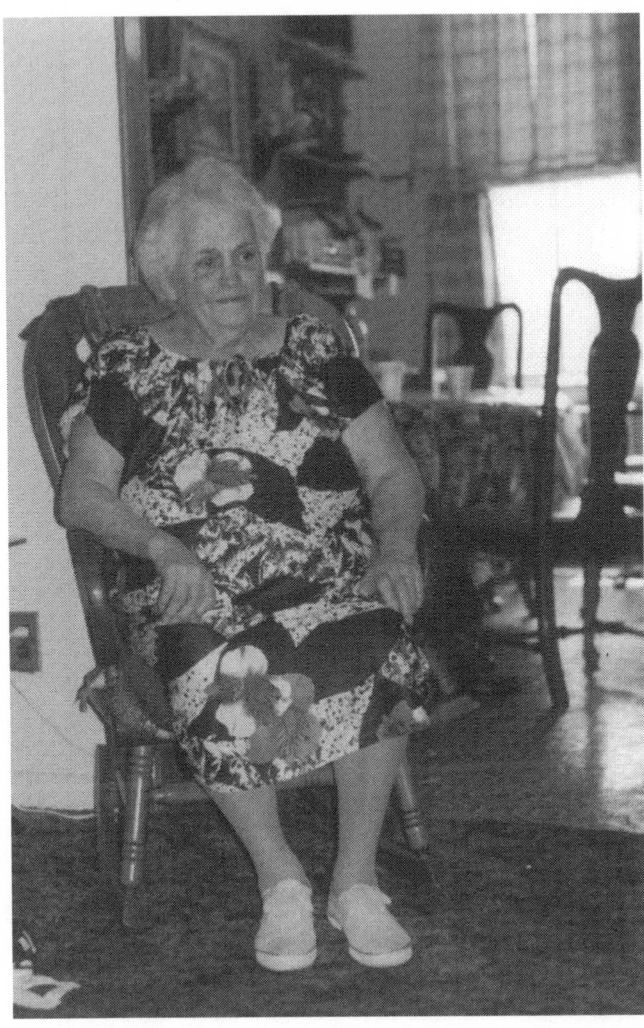

Connie, the sole survivor of Maria and Cono's eleven children,
tearfully reflects on the siblings she lost during her last visit to
145 Kingsland Avenue in 1996. She died at the age of eighty-four in 2001.

Ten of Maria and Cono's thirteen grandchildren gather for a farewell to the Carrano family homestead in 1996. They are holding up signs with the names of the three cousins who were not able to attend.

As I prepared to make my final departure, down the staircase where I said goodbye to my grandparents for the last time, I sat down and wrote a farewell to this building that had held host to the story of our lives:

The house stands vacant and dark now.

Our roots are buried deep in its foundation.

Soon we will be saying goodbye

To our past and the people we once were,

The people we loved who are long gone,

The trails of their laughter and singing,

The parties, the weddings.

It cradled mothers giving birth to children

And occupied children in their moments of play.

In this house generations grew up and grew old.

In this house our family has passed away,

Into sweet repose surrounded by its protective walls.

Looking out the window at the BQE.

Looking out and seeing the steeple of St. Cecilia's.

Looking down the block to see old friends

In the last of our days here after 100 years.

We're leaving the town where we first came,

Leaving the house after 60 years or more.

We're saying goodbye and closing the door,

Never to return forever more.

I went down the stairs and turned around. As I stood at the bottom of the dark stairwell, I looked up to the top of the second landing, brightly lit from the skylight above. "Goodbye, Nana … Goodbye, Grandpa." I turned around and went out the glass vestibule door.

A LIMB HAS FALLEN

A limb has fallen from the family tree,
I keep hearing a voice that says "Grieve not for me."
Remember the best times, the laughter, the song,
The good life I lived while I was strong.
Continue my heritage
I'm counting on you,
Keep smiling and surely the sun will shine through.
My mind is at ease, my soul is at rest,
Remembering all how I truly was blessed.
Continue traditions, no matter how small,

Go on with your life; don't just stare at the wall.
I miss you all dearly, so keep up your chin,
Until the day comes we are together again.

(Author Unknown)

HAPPY 90TH BIRTHDAY IN HEAVEN, NANA
September 15, 2004